Laughing Matter

LAUGHING MATTER

An Essay on the Comic

MARCEL GUTWIRTH

Cornell University Press

ITHACA AND LONDON

First published 1993 by Cornell University Press.

International Standard Book Number 0-8014-2783-5
Library of Congress Catalog Card Number 92-30520
Printed in the United States of America
*Librarians: Library of Congress cataloging information
appears on the last page of the book.*

⊗ The paper in this book meets the minimum requirements
of the American National Standard for Information
Sciences—Permanence of Paper for Printed
Library Materials, ANSI Z39.48-1984.

for Madelyn

uxori dulce ridenti

Qu'on ne dise pas que je n'ai rien dit de nouveau, la disposition des matières est nouvelle.

[Let no one say that I have said nothing new; the arrangement of the material is new.]

—Blaise Pascal, *Pensées*

Contents

Acknowledgments

The John Simon Guggenheim Memorial Foundation awarded a fellowship which, together with a grant from the National Humanities Center, allowed me to spend my 1985–86 sabbatic leave from Haverford College at Research Triangle in North Carolina, where the Humanities Center's superb research facilities and staff allowed me to do much of the reading needed for this book under the most favorable circumstances. A six-week stint at the Bibliothèque Nationale in Paris gave additional scope to my research into French and German sources. The librarians there, as well as at the Humanities Center (which draws on the ample resources of the libraries at Duke, Chapel Hill, and the State University of North Carolina at Raleigh) and those at Bryn Mawr and Haverford and at the Graduate School and University Center of the City University of New York and its neighboring New York Public Library, earned all my gratitude for their unstinting helpfulness.

To my friends and colleagues Wayne Booth at the University of Chicago, Gérard Defaux at the Johns Hopkins University, and Richard Bernstein at the New School for

Social Research, for their faith in my work, to which they lent their support when it was a mere grant proposal, and for their friendship over the years I give warm thanks.

Madelyn Gutwirth, to whom this book is dedicated in small return for a lifetime of shared pleasure in laughter, gave it a searchingly critical reading from which it emerged, though certainly not faultless, improved: a gift that beggars routine expression of gratitude.

M. G.

Laughing Matter

CHAPTER ONE

Laughter,
and Its Explicators

Trying to define humor is one of the definitions of humor.

—Saul Steinberg

Nothing is funny to everyone and anything seems potentially funny to someone.

—La Fave

To seek to give an account of the nature of laughter is to invite a stubborn resistance, made up in equal parts of a healthy skepticism and a perhaps no less healthy reluctance to know. We do not wish to have the secret of our spontaneity pried into. We take no pleasure in having it reduce to formula. Laughter, that least deliberate of explosions, is also our most valued reflex. Why grant another the right to hand us the key to it?

Take, on the other hand, Voltaire's mocking preamble to the article "Laughter" in his *Dictionnaire philosophique:* "Those who know why this kind of joy that kindles laughter should draw the zygomatic muscle—one of the thirteen muscles of the mouth—back toward the ears are knowing indeed." The very little we do know of the matter, though it manages to fill volumes, certainly helps bring home the sarcasm. Small wonder then that those rash enough to want to tell us why we laugh generally enter upon the matter on a note of propitiation.

For all that we are rightly reluctant and rightly skeptical, we are nonetheless curious. Though it may not be possible to give an unassailable account of why we laugh, any attempt to do so involves us in some sort of an analysis of human nature—and *that* is a topic we are by no means reluctant to pursue.

The "why" of "why we laugh" opens up three distinct avenues of inquiry, however, each of which has led to a set of answers that must be acknowledged in the construction of a would-be comprehensive explanation of the phenomenon of laughter.

The first set might aptly be labeled *functionalist*. It is made up of the views that look upon explanation as an account of the wherefore of laughter. They posit a purpose for the phenomenon, and they seek it in the function it is called upon to serve. Does laughter keep us in line? Does it help us to bond? Will it not keep the peace? In one way or another these accounts integrate laughter into a larger human enterprise.

A second set of answers clusters around the notion of an emotional benefit to the one who does the laughing. They are the so-called *psychological* theories, predicated each time on a specific trait that is allowed to stand for human nature. The best-known of these is the superiority theory associated with Thomas Hobbes, but three other subsets feature the motifs of degradation, relief, and play. In each case, laughter is accounted for by its presumed motivation.

A third set, finally, explains why we laugh with a rigorous description of what makes us laugh. These theories define laughter by its starting point, which they locate in the perception of an incongruity. Because they thus lay stress on its intellectual rather than its emotional character, they are referred to as *intellectualist*. We owe to them an understanding of the binary structure of the occasion of laughter, a structure that reflects its character as an "intellectual emotion," to use Claude Saulnier's telling phrase (34).

Theories of the comic thus parcel up among themselves a complex unitary phenomenon, in deference to one or another explanatory mode, to one or another concept of causation. It is my business in this book to arrive at a synthesis of these views, in an account of the nature of laughter that seeks to satisfy the three aspects of the adverb *why* that have been shown to preside jointly over the question, Why do we laugh?

*

"Le rire," pronounces Rabelais (after Aristotle),[1] "est le propre de l'homme" (Man is the laughing animal). That the claim can be made absolutely is open to dispute. That we should *want* to make it is at the heart of the matter. Alongside such capital attributes as language and tool making, laughter offers itself jocosely as of the essence, as definitional of the species. *Homo sapiens, Homo faber,* is also dressed up as *Homo ludens, Homo ridens.*

What of the claims of our lower brethren—lower, that is, on a scale of evolution of which we take ourselves to be the apex? Konrad Lorenz has a striking phrase, *tierischer Ernst* (animal earnestness), to convey our sense of the relentless in-dead-earnest that the necessity to feed and propagate and survive against great odds, preyed upon and preying, enforces on the animal kingdom. Next to that perception must be laid down the awareness that we know next to nothing of the inner life, which we blithely suppose nonexistent, of the inexorably silent majority that populates the

---

[1] "Monon gelan tōn zōōn anthrōpon" (human beings . . . being the only creatures that laugh): Aristotle, *Parts of Animals* 3.10.673a.9.

globe. Do ants quietly gesticulate their mirth, antenna to antenna? It would certainly violate the character we attribute to them, in fable or in monograph: but then, who spins the former, or pens the latter? Not the ant, surely. There is no getting out of that particular circle.

Another entryway is anecdote, notoriously seductive, notoriously unsound. Illustrious pet owners including Thomas Mann and Isak Dinesen vouch for their dogs' prankishness, their silent laughter. Quizzical Montaigne sticks in his oar: "When I play with my cat, am I playing with her, or is she playing with me?" Dinesen's tale, at any rate, is irresistible. Her deerhound Pania, having once stalked a treed serval cat successfully (the predator was shot), one day repeated the performance as her mistress returned empty-handed from a partridge hunt.

> I ran up to the tree. But, when I looked up, there was a black domestic cat sitting, very angry, as high up as possible in the swaying top of the tree. I lowered my gun. "Pania," I said, "you fool! It's a cat."
>
> As I turned round to Pania, he stood at a little distance, looking at me and splitting his sides with laughter. When his eyes met mine he rushed up to me, danced, wagged his tail, whined, put his feet on my shoulders, and his nose to my face, then jumped back again to give free course to his laughter.
>
> He expressed by pantomine: "I know. I know. It was a tame cat. I knew all the time. Indeed, you must excuse me. But if you only knew the figure you cut, rushing up to a tame cat with a gun! (287–88)

The case could not be put more vividly, or more unscientifically. We must leave it at that, fortified with a Delphic pronouncement on the matter from the pen of Robert M. Yerkes: "Probably most open-minded observers would unhesitatingly say either: I believe that the animals smile or laugh because I have seen them do so, or, I do not believe it because I have not seen it" (160).

A more tractable, if no more decisive, set of issues arises from the phylogeny of laughing and smiling. Rather than puzzling out the possible meaning *to the animal* of a sprightliness that to us suggests mirth, we may ask how far what we call in ourselves laughter and smiling may be traced to analogous mimicry in anthropoid apes. J. A. R. A. M. van Hooff advances the view that, though the baring of teeth "originally form[ed] part of a mainly defensive or protective pattern of behaviour, this element becomes a signal of submission and non-hostility" (Hinde 217). It is the appeasement display, of which I say more in the next chapter. Grist to the mill of those who look to primitive hostility for the roots of human laughter, you might think. Not, I hasten to make clear, so long as we wish to understand the only laughter that may be called properly human, the laughter that is the subject of our inquiry: the laughter of amusement. The venerable *argumentum de animalibus* (argument from the animals), as it always does, begs the question. Whatever survival value we may assign to the apish rictus in the economy of feral existence tells us no more about human laughter than that it can be bent to similar usage—as in the laughter of deference that greets the boss's unfunny quip. It tells us nothing regarding that "unwilling suspension of disbelief" (Charney) that leads us to "burst out" laughing when the punch line rings in.

"Humor," writes anthropologist Mahadev Apte, "provides the best evidence of the psychic unity of mankind" (261). As the disposition to be amused, humor thus binds all humankind into one by way of an Aristotelian universal. Laughter, in Aristotle's own formulation, defines our kind through its differentia (as against all other kinds, that is). For a reflex that has problematic standing in the Darwinian scheme of things, that is rather a large calling—the more so since contemporary anthropology so thoroughly mistrusts the transcultural generalizations dear to the age that fell under the spell of *The Golden Bough*. Nor must we lose sight of the fact that, though the laughter of amusement may resound from the pole to the equator, the occasion for it is rigorously circumstance- and situation-bound—that it is strictly local, in other words. In answer to the question put by a searching colleague, Is there not a source of laughter that cuts across time and place and language? one instance comes to mind, securely universal: the lurch of a drunk, familiar to all nations not unacquainted with alcohol. Utterly recognizable, utterly predictable, free of all verbal elaboration, standing therefore in no need of translation, the drunkard's progress, wildly overshooting its modest goal with each step taken, arms flailing helplessly, expends infinite pains to overcome nonexistent obstacles. Helpless in the grip of a condition pleasurably self-inflicted and no less easily remediable (sleep it off!), the inebriated sot is risible without a pang. No call for program notes: in a sequence of Kabuki dances, spellbinding but impenetrable to a Western audience, laughter rises secure as the stylized drunkard comes on.

Humor, thus trotted up in the attempt to make sense of laughter, appears to beg the question. I assign to it, at least for the time being, the function of standing in for the willingness and the capacity to be amused, as well as for the quality of that which amuses. The general term for the range of events, willed or unwilled, aimed at bringing amusement (or simply having that effect) is in these pages the *comic*. Nomenclature itself is a slippery issue, dotted with such unreliable cognates across Western languages alone as *Humor* (German), our *humor*, and, in French, *humour*.[2] Shading off wit from irony or delimiting such neigh-

[2] See Olivier Revault d'Allonnes's none-too-reliable tables of correspondence, in "Le comique, the comic, die Komik et la suite," *Revue d'Esthétique* 19 (1966): 364–74.

boring territories as satire, irony, and the grotesque seems less urgent, however, than doing justice to the bewildering variety discernible within the phenomenon of laughter itself, a variety that leads to the caveat about the unitary term *humor*. As we must recognize, it forms but one of the legitimate occasions for the irruption of laughter in daily life. Théodore Ribot, near the turn of the century, threw up his hands in despair at that unmanageable plenty: "Laughter manifests itself under conditions so heterogeneous and so numerous—physical sensations, joy, contrast, the bizarre, surprise, oddity, baseness—that the reduction of these causes to one seems problematic" (358). And when one reads of "the frequency [of laughter] in . . . [small] groups" as being "in some cases upward of one hundred fifty discrete instances . . . in an hour" (Fine 315), it is hard to escape the feeling that humor per se must be swamped in such an avalanche. Laughter, we know, may be apologetic, obsequious, it may translate to an uneasy grin, it may bid welcome, express relief or complicity, it may enliven a collaborative effort: such, at any rate, is the list Georges Bastide draws up in "Le rire et sa signification éthique." To this may be added the gamut of derision: sardonic, disdainful, contemptuous laughter and that of ill-natured mockery or naked triumph. The point is that laughter can be annexed to communicate a host of moods or intentions. As a subsidiary language it can be drawn into the business of sociability, but its specific character, undiluted, is that of an explosive response, wrung from us most often "before we know it," by the ludicrous in one of its compelling guises.[3]

Etienne Souriau draws another boundary line through the tangle of laughter's variety. Rather than distinguish, as I just did, laughter of amusement from the laughter that measures the whole range of sociability, Souriau posits

[3] Bear with me; the circle will be broken by and by.

laughter high and low along strictly aesthetic lines. What he terms *rire de base,* crude laughter, is a mere reflex, indifferent to human worth, undemanding of fitness or justice. Anyone may be made laughable, any belief may be ridiculed. To accede to the comic proper, laughter must be tamed by art, for "the comic . . . is the direct opposite of the risible." It exorcises the "demon of laughter . . . , yanking out its viper's fangs, teaching it to dance—at the end of a stick" (151). Though such a resolutely high-minded outlook risks sundering the art of the comic from the *vis comica,* from the dark energies of laughter, it does help caution against the urge, ever present in the bosom of an author on any topic, to magnify his or her chosen theme, to paint it in the bright hues of a beneficence it does not possess. Much as we prize it, justifiably, laughter is not all bounty: it has its dark, its killing side. Art alone cannot render it harmless; think of the hapless recipient of a Voltairian or Johnsonian barb. Violence of some degree may well be of its essence, though held in check.

The physicality of laughter is another aspect of its mystery. That a respiratory spasm with vocal accompaniment should signify that an event—visual or auditory, verbal or gestural—has been "taken in" by consciousness raises the vexed specter of the mind-body problem. Still, in the physiology of laughter may be grasped the elements of at least a partial account of the global phenomenon. The pathological condition known as neonatal onset (laughter of the newborn) "demonstrates that brain substrates for laughter are fully functional at birth" (Duchowny 98), thus establishing the preexistence of a mechanism set to respond to a stimulation unlikely to occur before the fourth month of life (Sroufe and Wunsch 1326). Laughter is thus rooted in our physical makeup, and we must therefore look on it as fundamental to human nature. As separable, on the other hand, from the occasion of its characteristic onset in amusement, it is, as we have seen, capable of other—multi-farious—employment. Physiology thus restates, with heightened emphasis, both the centrality and the elusiveness of the phenomenon.

Another shaft of light issuing from the domain of physiology plays on the relationship of laughter to the smile. Though they may arise from phylogenetically distinct lines (van Hooff 277), the two appear to have converged in the course of evolution to form the two ends of a continuum of amusement. Smiling encompasses "the more voluntary phenomena of facial expression," laughter "the more automatic laryngeal and respiratory phenomena" (Ironside 589). The smile may thus be said to lend itself to the more deliberate expression and communication of positive or euphoric feelings, whereas laughter represents the explosive outcome of such a communication *received*. We smile, in other words, when we recognize that something is amusing, but we aren't helpless in the throes of that mild seizure we call laughter. The smile is a signal of our pleasure, not the irresistible surrender to it. As such it is peculiarly well adapted to function as body language, as the facial unspoken expression of good will first lavished by the mother upon her baby with an accompaniment of soothing sounds, grounding in first infancy the notion of love and trust.[4] The chuckles and gurgles of infant laughter, as an expression of correlative well-being, close the circle of euphoria within which amusement thrives. Thus, whether primarily expressive or primarily communicative, laughter (under which, for convenience, I subsume the smile)[5] corresponds to the positive range of emotional coloration.

---

[4] "With the mother smiling at the child in her arms and the child looking up in the mother's face and smiling back, human communication was born and facial expression originated" (Martin Grotjahn 258).

[5] The capacity to smile, like the ability to laugh, appears to be innate: "The deaf-blind reported in the literature smile," writes D. G. Freedman

Whether or not it is received as affirmative or life en-
hancing (by the butt, let us say), it is felt as such by the
one who is making merry. Norman Cousins and Joseph
Heller are among the more illustrious recent patients who
have testified in print to the curative virtues of laughter
taken in large doses at a critical juncture of their medical
histories.[6] Enid Welsford reports that "in 1498 Alfonso
d'Este fell seriously ill, and Isabelle [of Castille] sent her
favourite fool to cheer him. His success was amazing"
(132). Psychosomatic medicine, one can readily see, is but a
new label on an old bottle. Whether we take the view laid
down by Cousins that as the negative emotions detract
from well-being so the positive ones are apt to promote it;
or whether we endorse the more directly physiological approach of the physician James Walsh, who credits laughter
with "expos[ing] the blood to three or four times as much
oxydation at least as does quiet respiration" (29) and with
vigorously massaging inner organs by the up-and-down
motion of the diaphragm in hearty guffaws; or, again,
whether we heed the opening dedication of the fourth part
of Pantagruel's adventures, in which the physician Rabelais
cites Hippocrates and Galen in support of the doctor's primary obligation to rejoice the patient and lift up his drooping spirits by a joyous countenance, scientific speculation
meets up with folk wisdom in the confident identification
of laughter with health and well-being.

Physiology opens up still another avenue of understanding. A. Soulairac, in his contribution to Dr. André Berge et
al.'s *Introduction à l'étude scientifique du rire*, posits the ante-

---

(178). The same authority "closely observed one infant whose first social
smile, i.e. smiling with his eyes on the caretaker's face, occurred at 3 days
of age" (180).

[6] Norman Cousins, *Anatomy of an Illness as Perceived by a Patient* (New
York: Norton, 1979); Joseph Heller, *No Laughing Matter* (New York: Putnam, 1986).

rior portion of the hypothalamus as the seat of "relaxation of muscle tone and of reactions of contentment," whereas "the excitation of the posterior portion provokes an augmentation of motor excitability and reactions of rage" (68).[7] Laughter can occur, under these conditions, only when the tension brought about by a violent emotion has disappeared: "There [then] occurs a phenomenon of liberation which permits laughter to take place" (69). That, physiologically, laughter takes place under conditions of euphoria and relaxation, that it represents, in fact, a state of the organism in which the guard is down, is a matter of simple observation. We see that fact take its place principally in the theories of the comic reviewed in Chapter 3, which base explanation in psychology. The net result, however, is that in laughter the body is defenseless. The other side of that physical vulnerability is the mental security, the sense of confidence that allows the organism to let down its guard so entirely—eyes streaming, chest heaving, members limp with uncontrollable hilarity. This may be but another name for euphoria, but it singularly reinforces the connection with laughter of a state of well-being which not only flows from laughter and the good fellowship it promotes, the high spirits it releases, but appears in this latter consideration as the condition sine qua non of its full manifestation.

Two further observations throw into high relief the global character of the phenomenon. Soulairac, Ironside, Duchowny all make clear the involvement of both the cortex and the hypothalamus in the brain circuitry of laughter. Voluntary and involuntary impulses, mental and emotional factors, thus enter into the onset of hilarity. Additionally, in her contribution to the *Handbook of Humor Research* Vera Robinson writes: "Findings indicate . . . that laughter stim-

[7] Michael Duchowny, on the other hand, refers to the posterior hypothalamus as "a region of importance for both laughter and sexual maturation" (100).

ulate[s] both hemispheres at the same time, coordinating all senses and producing a unique level of consciousness and a high level mode of the brain processing. . . . In relation to psychotherapy, it affords the client the ability to see both the logical, concrete and the abstract or subtle nuances of his problem" (2:118–9). Paul E. McGhee, citing the identical research by S. Svebak, speaks of "integration of cognitive opposites" and goes on to use Svebak's own words: "A coordination of otherwise separate processes is typical in humor appreciation, and these processes seem to reflect the two functional modes attributed to each of the hemi- spheres" (*Handbook*, 2:18). Bilateralism on the one hand, cortico-hypothalamic involvement on the other, appear to vindicate both Saulnier's description of laughter as an intel- lectual emotion and Aristotle's attribution of it to human- kind alone, tapping as it does the resources of the human brain side to side and front to aft.

One last word about the physical side of laughter: it is infectious. Laughter sparks laughter. Conversely, a sober- sides companion mutes one's own mirth. Kate Osborne and Antony Chapman measured frequency and duration of adolescent laughter of solitary subjects and of subjects ac- companied by a responsive or an unresponsive companion; they found it practically suppressed in the third case, mea- surably enhanced in the second.[8] I recall a scene in an old Laurel and Hardy film, on the other hand, in which whey- faced Stan Laurel, for no reason at all, begins to giggle, then to laugh, then to hold his sides in inexplicable mirth. The audience, bemused at first, begins tentatively to join in the laughter, which soon turns into a pandemonium of uncontrollable hilarity that subsides with some difficulty, in time to hear the principal confess, under prodding from

[8] Kate Osborn and Antony Chapman, "Suppression of Adult Laughter: An Experimental Approach" (Chapman and Foot, *Funny Thing* 429–43).

impatient Oliver, that he has been laughing for no reason at all. And we've all had the experience of reading a joke that amuses us moderately, retelling it to a companion or a crowd, and laughing much harder for the hilarity it provokes in others, each in fact shaken reflexively by the mirth of the other, till both, or all, collapse helplessly in a heap of spent breath. The pygmies, we are told, laugh thus till they fall to the ground; it is hard to picture this happening to a pygmy unaccompanied and unabetted, in solipsistic jocularity. At all events, the contagion of laughter—sometimes, as in the epidemic of laughter among convent girls in Africa some years back, starkly hysterical[9]—lends easy credence to the contention that laughter is of its essence *convivial*, as Jean Fourastié puts it (66), that is to say, when all is said and done, human.

"Why is it that no one tickles himself?" inquires Aristotle in his *Problems* (2:965a6). "Is it not," he goes on to suggest, "because one is tickled less even by another when the act is expected, so that the effect is minimized when one is aware of the experience? Laughter is a sort of surprise and deception." Aristotle, as usual, has put his finger on a moot question on the borderline between purely physical reflex laughter, such as could be set off by electrical stimulation of an appropriate region of the brain, and the laughter of amusement, Saulnier's intellectual emotion. The answer to the question posed, however, may have to be looked for beyond the issue of anticipation and lack of surprise. The role of surprise, as I argue in a later chapter, is not a simple one in the realm of the comic: anticipation, in some cases, may be compatible with it, may even render it more effective. This may in fact be the case in the tickling of an infant, where a slow buildup of anticipatory excitement lends the force of a paroxysm—of shrieking delight, cas-

---

[9] Reported by T. A. Lambo, as cited in Frederic R. Stearns, *Laughing* 40.

cading into laughter—to the dreaded tickle when at last it occurs. Frederic Stearns cites a study by B. A. Houssay which distinguishes tickling of two kinds: "One is caused by deep repeated pressure at 'adequate' intervals in certain areas such as armpits, thorax, thigh. The other one is produced by light intermittent cutaneous stimuli or 'by successive stimulation of adjacent spots at low intensity.' Houssay contends that this second type of tickle is due to 'simultaneous excitation of touch and pain receptors'"(4). It is not inconceivable that one might tickle oneself in the second manner, with the help, say, of a feather, achieving, if not laughter, at least a mild diversion. What would be missing, and could by no means be spared with regard to tickling of the first kind, is the playful ambiance of mock-aggression that is inseparable from a tickling session. In the mixture of pain and pleasure that mock-aggression implies, the two kinds (by virtue of Houssay's observation) are at one. Tickling may be viewed as an attack that melts into a caress. The too rapid oscillation of contradictory sensations, taken together with the alternation of pressure and release that is tickling itself, triggers the equally spasmodic reflex of helpless laughter, as consciousness is flooded with contradictions it cannot afford to give up on. Prolonged unduly, the spasms turn to difficulty in getting one's breath, the helplessness turns to panic: the threshold of pleasure is crossed into pain. Amusement thus turned to dismay reflects quite instructively what must be recognized as of the essence of genuine laughter, that it is unforced. Laughter is so much the truest expression of our spontaneity that we hate to see it weighed down with the shackles of explanation. To tickle beyond comfort curtails that very liberty of which laughter is the unfettered expression.

We may have come full circle, back to Aristotle's rash claim that laughter differentiates between human and animal nature. Liberty is but another name for the specifically human indeterminacy that fetters us to no machinery of instinct. Wired for laughter from very birth, we appear to have evolved the capacity to laugh from no other motive than a pleasurable surprise that serves no end but the enjoyment of our own momentary invulnerability in euphoria. Whether or not we choose to define human nature by its capacity for amusement, laughter stands as the audible and visible sign of what in that nature we most particularly prize.

The vast domain of the comic is the welter of all the occasions that, potentially or actually, move to laughter—a definition as elastic as it is tautological. No better one is on the horizon, it seems. A glance at the two epigraphs heading this chapter supplies a hint of that condition. Three authorities, writing in three languages, lend their weight to the observation. Siegfried J. Schmidt writes, "I am certain that, on specifiable grounds, no definition in any rigorous scientific-theoretical sense of definition can be given of it" (166). Jean Fourastié writes that, "in the matter of laughter, we can only find conditions that are necessary *in general*, and conditions that are *often* sufficient" (182). Quintilian, however, had already put it with the lapidary succinctness proper to classical Latin: "Primum itaque considerandum est, et quis et in qua causa, et apud quem et in quem et quid dicat" (*Institutio oratoria* 6.3.28): in seeking to evaluate a jest, we must consider who speaks, in what cause, before whom, against whom, and to what effect. Every circumstance weighs in; laughter cannot be moved "in general," nor can a particular occurrence guarantee, under seemingly identical conditions and before an identical public, a recurrence of equal force. These observations tend to support the view that the business of a general definition of the comic is an idle one. No immutable definition of life exists,

Saint Augustine confessed that he knew well enough what time was, until asked about it, and Mr. Justice Potter Stewart unforgettably "defined" pornography by saying, "I can't tell what it is, but I know it when I see it." It seems wise therefore to proceed with no more than a tautological definition of the comic as that which moves to amused laughter until we run down the major families of theoretical formulations that aim to give us a less provisional understanding of it.

Folly may well be the widest possible category we can apply to capture something of the variegation of the comic. The word, in English, is almost too encompassing, designating indifferently as it does excess and deficiency. At one end of the spectrum it corresponds to the French *sottise*, the Latin *stultitia*, denoting what we would call foolishness. At the other end it takes in *folie* or *mania*, which in English is madness. Erasmus, in his *Moriae encomium*, or *Laus stultitiae*, veers freely from one to the other, ranging over the whole gamut of the irrational (at a time when the absurd did not yet rate a capital). Institutionalized in the court jester, who wears motley, sports cap and bells, brandishing a bauble; near-deified in the trickster figure of native American myth; taking to the boards as Pierrot or Harlequin; infiltrating epic and romance as Reynard, Eulenspiegel, Panurge, or Simplicissimus; surviving marginally as circus clown, centrally as stand-up comic—the Fool is as versatile as he is immortally ubiquitous, popping up now as Ubu *roi*, now as Sad Sack, Mortimer Snerd, or Donald Duck.

Let us picture the Fool in action, in a scene primitive enough to catch out the comic in its farcical bare bones. Making a rush at the crowd, he gooses a spectator with his bauble. The mitigated aggression, the jerky reflex action of mild bodily disarray, provide matter for hearty laughter. What is that spectator to do to escape confusion? Stylizing his dismay, he participates in the exhibition rather than merely undergoing it as its target. He thereby takes on the comic role instead of having it foisted on him. The jerkiness of an unwilled reflex endures in the willed, in the artful representation of it, but no longer pertains to his physique alone. He joins in in the carefree enjoyment of a body subject to reflex motion, capable of momentary disorganization. He shares in the laughter.

Two distinct modes of the comic correspond to the two phases of that pantomime: the *infliction* of ridicule, not unmixed with derision, in which laughter is invited at a victim's expense; a prankish *communion* in shared finitude, not unmixed in this case with admiration for the art that turns a fall into a leap, beholden to the spirit of mirth. Both figure in varying proportions in most occurrences of the comic, and neither should be taken as sole explanation of the phenomenon—a counsel of inclusiveness too often honored in the breach.

Another way to begin to delimit the domain of the risible is to ask, Where does laughter stop? Under what conditions is it not only impermissible but unthinkable to laugh? We know that laughter is inhibited by rage or pain, that is, by any overwhelming emotion, practically by definition. Short, however, of the kind of compassion that turns the pain of another into felt pain, or the kind of fear that freezes the laughter on our lips—the pity and terror of Aristotle's definition of tragedy—laughter is rigorously incompatible with awe. Awesomeness and absurdity are two distinct perspectives: we cannot encompass them simultaneously. Zeus must set aside his majesty as the father of the gods to consort with Alcmena in the figure of her husband, Amphitryo. The prank of a god in bed with a mortal under the features of that mortal's husband requires either that we cease to believe in his divinity or that it get in no one's but Amphitryo's way. The ease, in fact, with which Homeric religion slides in and out of a sense of the gods' divinity marks it as possessed of a freedom from awe we can no longer fully understand. Laughter is not out of place on Mount Olympus—the gods have their fill of it at lame Hephaistos as he bustles about serving the drinks; and we mere mortals join in at the discomfiture of faithless Aphrodite, caught in a net of her husband's devising while disporting herself in bed with hateful Ares. The lesson, if there is one to be drawn from such freedom, is that awe is an emotion we must not overdo. The sublime, the French remind us, is but a step away from the ridiculous. That step is soon taken when we trade genuine awe for mere solemnity. As a species of self-importance, the latter falls under the sway of the comic; for the ground utterly forbidden to laughter, when all is said and done, is and must remain no more than a tiny enclave—or else we give up to the Malvolios of existence far more than cakes and ale.

A spirited passage by Harvey Mindess in *Laughter and Liberation* returns us to our starting point by setting on Aristotle's proud claim of our uniqueness as laughing species the seal of tongue-in-cheek approval: "It is not by accident that man is the only animal who has a sense of humor. He is also the only animal who wears clothing, denies himself sex, worships non-existent deities, starves in order to create, kills and dies for his country, slaves and cheats for his bank balance. Clearly, he is the only animal who *needs* a sense of humor" (25).

*

One of the liveliest and in many ways soundest works on the comic remains Max Eastman's *Enjoyment of Laughter*, for all that it strains a bit too desperately, at times, for the jocular. In approaching the quirks and biases of theoreticians themselves, it might not be amiss to quote from a chapter jauntily titled "Eddie Cantor on the Auction Block":

What deters us from taking up jocular analysis as a profession is not the difficulty inherent in the job, but the fact that when the job is well done, nobody gets any fun out of it. The correct explanation of a joke not only does not sound funny, but it does not sound like a correct explanation. It consists of imagining ourselves totally humorless and most anxiously and minutely concerned with the matter in question, and in realizing that under those queer and uninteresting circumstances a disagreeable feeling *would* arise exactly where in our mirthful receptivity we experience a comic emotion. That is not funny, and except to the pure love of understanding, it is not fun. (41)

The trite and generally self-defensive observation that theorizing about the comic is not itself an activity productive of mirth (although certainly open to ridicule) is not the main burden of this paragraph. What it admirably catches up is that *the stance* of explanation brackets and removes from consideration the matter to be explained, that to duplicate the moment of humorous apperception humorlessly is to seek to understand running by first lopping off one's feet. To say that to engage in explanation isn't fun, except to the mind, "the pure love of understanding," is to say little, since it is in an activity of the mind, in the eager quest for understanding, that the theoretician engages. To say that the quest consists of first evacuating the object of the search, of imagining it under conditions that preclude its being recognized, is to undercut the whole enterprise more seriously.

Yet if to explain a joke may well be the futile exercise Eastman takes it for, the job of the theoretician does not quite amount to that. That job has more to do with laying down the conditions under which the comic operates and specifying the view of human nature these conditions imply.

Such at any rate is the logical sequence that can be

posited in the abstract. The fact of the matter is that the explicator, be he Hobbes or Bergson or Freud, invariably proceeds from a firmly held view of human nature, which an explanation of the nature and causes of laughter is called upon to buttress. Bacon's inductive method has long since been recognized as having little application to a description of the procedures of natural scientists. They do not sit around making observations that build up to a hypothesis; rather, they seek confirmation of the hypothesis sparked by perhaps no more than a single observation in further experiments designed to yield appropriate supporting evidence. Likewise those who investigate the nature of laughter scarcely ever approach their subject unprompted by some general thesis with regard to its place in human affairs, which dictates a specific configuration corroborated by selective observation. No certainties emerge in that notoriously indeterminate terrain: we seek our footing in probabilities that, at best, turn into plausibilities.[10] When we consider further that explanations of laughter arise in a variety of domains of intellectual inquiry, ranging from cultural anthropology to theory of literature, by way of psychology and sociology, we come to the realization that whole fields of learning complete with postulates and assumptions of their own enter into the equation. A look first at the explicators themselves appears to be urgently in order.

We find, ranged on either side of an impassable ditch, the rationalists and the irrationalists—the partisans, that is, of an orderly universe in which laughter is but a passing disturbance, and the proponents of a wilder, more risk-loving scheme with which laughter is wholly in tune. Marie Collins Swabey gives clearest utterance to the first view.

[10] See Alasdair MacIntyre, "The Character of Generalizations in Social Science and Their Lack of Predictive Power," in *After Virtue* chap. 8.

Morton Gurewitch is the flamboyant spokesman of the
second. For Swabey "it is the perception of a local incongruity as incapable of truth or reality . . . that affords the
basic satisfaction of a comic perception" (13). Laughter
salutes the vindication of reason: though briefly unhorsed,
it is soon back in the saddle, reins held high. Not momentary error but "the *correction* of an error by the understanding gives satisfaction as making for the victory of reason
over unreason in the world" (107). In this view, which is
that of philosophical idealism, the comic is no more than a
minor disturbance, a momentary stumble, which affords
the pleasurable emotion of a setting to rights of what had
been briefly disarrayed: reason's calm composure ruling out
all unseemliness.

Gurewitch, in a book significantly titled *Comedy: The
Irrational Vision,* though he does not tackle Swabey head
on certainly gives ample service to an opposing truth. A
"drive to celebrate irrationalism" lies at the back of much
comedy, he asserts. Comedy's "interest in illogic and irrev-
erence" must therefore be taken as the proper focus of
investigation (9). A figure like Alfred Jarry's Ubu is seen as
catching up perfectly the raucous wildness of laughter.
Gurewitch writes that Ubu "emblematizes both the incubus
of society and the diabolism of history by farcically ex-
emplifying the predatory and lunatic patterns of each. And
as decent citizens we can only detest his infamy. But insofar as we are wanton children and ingrained immoralists,
we enjoy Ubu's vast disintegration of controls; for Ubu is
also the beast from the id" (159–60). The energy of the style
gives it away: laughter is, in this view, as is the poet for
Blake, of the party of the devil, rejoicing in undreamt-of
upheaval and vividly imagined anarchy.

In the ranks behind Swabey we may number such disparate figures as Hegel and Bergson. Idealism certainly
predisposes a thinker like Hegel to look on laughter as an

irreverent disruption so fully overcome as to afford sovereign reason the brief elation of having set matters to rights. Bergson's vitalism, on the other hand, paints the comic as a momentary lapse of organic fluidity into mechanical rigidities, *du mécanique plaqué sur du vivant*. Siding against the intrusive disruption, Bergson finds in laughter a reassertion of the rightness of the adaptive, driving the eccentric out of bounds.

Gurewitch too is in eminent company: Schopenhauer, oddly enough, whose idealism has in it a nihilistic strain and who finds the laugher rejoicing to discover, for once, "this strict untiring, and most troublesome governess, the reason . . . convicted of inadequacy" (2:98), as abstract principles stumble on the hard rock of the particular perceptions. Nietzsche thus finds himself in unlikely fellowship with his philosophical bête noire in his own not unexpected canonization of laughter as the salutary cure for the aberrations of pure reason. George Santayana, apostle of an unfettered spiritual freedom, saw in the comic the truest expression of the inherently anarchic reality of existence, "a conjunction of things mutually irrelevant, a chapter of accidents, a medley improvised here and now for no reason, to the exclusion of the myriad other farces which, so far as their ideal structure is concerned, might have been performed just as well" (142). Contingency, which dictated to Sartre's Roquentin the nightmare of an absurd proliferation, rings to Santayana the peals of universal laughter.

Santayana's laughter and Roquentin's dismay at a Creation which both take to be unremittingly contingent offer confirmation that one's stance in the face of irreducible difference is rooted ultimately in temperament. We may align laughter with reason triumphant if we choose, or we may look upon it as the sign that reason on this occasion stumbled and had to pick itself up unhurt from whatever floor it walks on. The matter cannot be decided by an appeal to fact or reason. It comes down to a leap of faith, on the side of either reason or unreason. Skeptics will wager on the one, dogmatists on the other. Whichever "truth" we choose, our theory will promote. Human nature, that notoriously elastic construct, is to be discovered at either end of the theorizing process: it goes in as a premise and comes out, discernibly fortified, as a conclusion—a circularity that is not so uncommon in the study of human affairs, but against the likelihood of which it is good to proceed forearmed.

A look at the disciplines importantly represented in the field of comic theory reveals certain significant groupings. Sociology and anthropology make their appearance marching to the drum of Darwinian natural selection. The dimension of laughter that marks it off as a social phenomenon is given pride of place; the possibility that it could arise outside a social context, visible or implied, rejected out of hand. Anthropology, moreover, seeks out those occasions for laughter that distinguish one culture from another and fastens particularly on the role of the ritual clown. His deliberate reversal of accepted behavior helps to define the norms more rigorously. At the same time, it represents a kind of delegation of the power to ward off by direct contact the chaos the taboos are supposed to contain. By thus harnessing the power of laughter to their special concerns, these two disciplines operate in conformity with the general model set for the sciences of life by the Darwinian postulate of natural selection. All features of existence are accountable to this high tribunal for their presence in a viable organism, be it social or unitary. All must show cause for merely being there, on the ground of superior adaptivity. Hence laughter, that supremely gratuitous manifestation, finds itself hauled perforce into the service of social integration or cultural survival. Functionality is the keynote sounded by the theories that make their home in the social sciences.

Another set of explicators gather under the umbrella of

Value. They are the moralists, the theologians, the aestheticians. An account of laughter tinged with reprobation tends to emerge from that quarter. Etienne Souriau's invidious distinction between aesthetic laughter, refined by art, and the crude garden variety is an instance of the distrust in which the phenomenon is held by those who revere higher sensibilities or a more exalted Being. Lord Chesterfield disapproved of laughter's vulgarity. Baudelaire saw in it the mark of the Fall, a manifestation of man's monstrous pride. Bishop Bossuet excoriated it in the name of the fathers of the church, ringing in the scriptural admonition *vae ridentibus*, woe unto those who laugh.

In the hierarchy of literary genres, comedy is seldom set on a par with tragedy as an expression of what is most profound in human nature. Among the practitioners of the genre, in fact, few rise above the trivializing possibilities inherent in it, thereby reinforcing the prejudices of the theoreticians. The prejudicial opposition of laughter and seriousness has its roots in this state of mind, which may be no more than the generalized impatience nurtured by laughter's challenge to all established, all unquestioned values. However that may be, a strain of outright rejection must be reckoned into the assessment of laughter as a feature of human behavior worthy of study and deserving of estimation.

The place of the study of laughter in a systematic summation of the human condition is another, quite fundamental, explicator of an explicator's conclusions. Take the case of Hobbes. We owe to his pen one of the most incisive, as well as the most influential, definitions of laughter, as "a *sudden glory* arising from some sudden *conception* of some *eminency* in ourselves, by *comparison* with the *infirmity* of others, or with our own formerly" (chap. 9.13). It takes little reflection to perceive how well this formulation fits the Hobbesian view of human nature as the arena of a merciless struggle of all against all, how in fact it offers a stunning *raccourci* of that very outlook. In like manner we cannot escape the realization that *du mécanique plaqué sur du vivant* vividly confirms Bergson's vitalistic advocacy of the organic as the supremely adaptive, or that the Victorian thinker Alexander Bain's characterization of the comic as "the degradation of a person or interest having dignity" (4.39) neatly suits the Victorian scheme of things, in which dignity mightily prevails. The study of laughter, in other words, often takes place along the margins of more comprehensive or more exalted preoccupations: it lodges where it can on the outskirts of a mighty systematic construct, taking on the general coloration of the whole. The explanation thus furnished of the meaning of the phenomenon is apt therefore to partake of whatever weaknesses may be detected in the system as a whole.

Then there are the psychologists. As the science that embraces the phenomena of human perception and of human intellection in its jurisdiction, psychology, in the heyday of behaviorism, has had little to say about laughter, leaving its study at the point to which Spencer and Freud had taken it, viewed as a pleasurable dissipation of energy accumulated to some end that did not materialize. Greater effort has since been devoted, in the past quarter of a century, to a quantified approach based on more up-to-date views of the nervous system, such as degrees of arousal or volume of information, but most studies preface their experimental data with a justified lament at the rudimentary state of our information or at the paradox of evoking (and measuring) laughter under laboratory conditions. The theses offered for such experimental verification have by and large been developed by those who labor outside the precincts ruled by quantification, and the self-evident limitations placed on the understanding of a phenomenon such as laughter by strict measurement must be given their due when one considers the paucity of solid information yielded.

Finally, this survey, which makes no claim to exhaustiveness, may come to rest in the domain of literary criticism. Here, generally, we deal with theory of comedy for which, paradoxically, the first impulse is given by the failure of Aristotle's *Poetics* to bring out the nature of comedy as intriguingly and in as great detail as that of tragedy. Much is made, following Aristotle's lead, of the possible origins of comedy in a phallic processional, slanging match, or satyr dance. Much will be made also, following the model of Menander's plays, the so-called New Comedy, of comedy's faithfulness to middling circumstances of existence, its mirroring of everyday reality. More recently the accent has fallen on fertility ritual and folklore (Cornford) or carnival exuberance (Bakhtin), while Northrop Frye postulates for the comedy's denouement the coming together of a society made afresh, a brave new world prepared for a redemptive future. All of this may be seen to suggest a resolutely life-affirming bias and an emphasis on the euphoric, if not downright manic, dimension of the art sustained by our capacity for laughter and our wish to see it exercised. Some, to be sure, unwilling to confound the comedic and the hilarious, insist that laughter is not the significant mark of a successful comedy, where much else—romance, fantasy, gentle irony—hangs in the balance. A comedy that does not at any point amuse, however, the "tearful comedy" devised by eighteenth-century sentiment, ruling the air waves at midday in twentieth-century soap operas, appears to most of us to usurp the name of comedy, smuggling into our parlors instead the eternal loops of romance. The theorists of comedy thus bring to the study of laughter a perspective shaped both by history and by a set of special circumstances to which they must be held accountable. Though these may act as both access and limitation, inevitably they narrow our understanding of laughter to the requirements of a particular craft.

∗

A *New Yorker* cartoon some years back (by Peter Arno, I believe) showed two monks earnestly devising. One turned to the other, and the caption read, "But I *am* holier than thou." It raised more than a smile to my lips, as I remember; in all likelihood a hearty chuckle.

How to account for it?

I see in it first of all a switch. We viewer-readers undergo a reversal of expectations, perhaps two. The sight of monks in their corded habits may raise in our minds thoughts of serenity in meditation, which the caption rudely pulls back to earth—but the likelihood of that particular disappointment is diminished by the cartoon setting, with *its* attendant expectations. Not so in the case of the switch from the standard admonition "Don't you be so holier than thou!" to the blithe assertion in the caption: it offers an indisputable reversal.

The reversal upends a standard expectation, that we not take ourselves as better than our fellows. Is it too much to speak of it as the counsel of wisdom? Though merely workaday, let it stand here in the place of that noble entity, reason. We laugh, then, in this case, to see reason, which we prize, unceremoniously brushed aside by folly, which we misprize: a victory of the worse over the better.

Much remains to be filled in. Do we misprize folly altogether, and at all times? How is the effect achieved? How does the monk, how does Arno get away with it? Would we laugh at all if we held the cloistered life dear and the contemplative ideal wholly sanctified—if, in other words, we felt it all too close for comfort? And what of the impulse that invites us to rejoice in the frailties of others? Hobbes, Descartes, Kant, Freud, and many others are called to the rescue in the coming chapters to go beyond this skeletal outline.

A few things may be clear already. The view of the comic to which I subscribe implies the defeat, though brief and inconsequential, of that which we normally honor, which for convenience I call reason. It ranges me therefore with the irrationalists, though I rejoice in the defeat of reason in laughter solely because it is brief and unenduring. My chuckle at Arno's visual bon mot leaves my respect for barefoot monks unimpaired. Nor am I tempted to scoff at either holiness or humility for having seen them set at odds in a mock-plausible display. My view allows for the subversiveness of laughter as a subversiveness that manages to exact no price. Clearly I side with the upholders of incongruity as a starting point. Clearly I subscribe to the (mitigated) violence the comic is supposed to wreak on persons or institutions. And those two "clearly's" range me with Thomas Hobbes on the one hand and Alexander Bain on the other, without my altogether sharing the views of either. The tale of the next three chapters, in fact, is the tale of the variety of approaches to the question of the comic with which for the most part I find myself in partial agreement, and out of which I seek to fashion an account comprehensive enough to merit a place in the series.

CHAPTER TWO

Laughter Conscripted:
A Socio-Integrative Approach

Haec enim ridentur vel sola vel maxime quae notant et designant
turpitudinem aliquam non turpiter. [An indecency decently put is
the thing we laugh at hardest.]

—Cicero

As late as the eighteenth century the professors of German universities could augment their income by playing the fool at court.

—Enid Welsford

When in the *Poetics* Aristotle gives as the proper
object of comedy "the imitation of characters of a lower
type [*phauloterōn*]," he specifies that they are not to be
taken as "in the full sense of the word bad [*kakian*], . . .
the Ludicrous being merely a subdivision of the ugly [*tou
aischrou*]." He goes on to complete the definition of the
ludicrous, sharpening it by example: "It consists in some
defect or ugliness which is not painful or destructive. To
take an obvious example, the comic mask is ugly and distorted, but does not imply pain" (5.1).

Absence of pain may well be the most arguable as well
as the most valuable element in this definition, but more
far-reaching in its bearing on the history of the subject is
the judgment it delivers on the ludicrous as a subspecies of
the ugly. Embedded in a discussion of tragedy, the few

remarks that pertain to comedy partake of the character of antithesis. Tragedy elevates, idealizes its personnel; comedy depreciates or caricatures the human race. The one genre depicts our betters, the other those we feel able to look down upon, our moral and social inferiors—morally inferior because they *are* socially inferior. Clearly the definition opens the door to a lot of mischief: undervaluing the one art and disparaging ordinary humankind. Yet the importance of that almost offhand dismissal lies in two little-remarked assumptions that underlie it: first, that the path to an understanding of the comic lies in the assessment of the quality, of the worth of what we laugh at; second, that what we laugh at falls below the norm, that it is a failure of worth, a quality impaired. Underlying these two assumptions is the belief that laughter, to be understood, must be inserted in a social context, that it discriminates between such socially arrived-at judgments as the fair and the ugly, the better and the worse, the successful and the failed. Though Aristotle did not spell out his assumptions or draw any general conclusions, his influential formulation established a context within which matters relating to an understanding of comedy easily lined up under consideration of social utility measured on a scale socially preordained.

A first consequence of this functional bias, which directed comic theory toward an assessment of how well laughter serves social ends, was to set the framework in which comedy as a genre was analyzed and described well into the late eighteenth century.

George McFadden aptly translates my epigraph from Cicero's *De oratore* as "the presentation of something offensive in an inoffensive manner" (56). Though it is concerned with the appropriate use of facetiousness in legal or political oratory and thus falls into the province of rhetoric rather than that of aesthetics, this formulation partakes of the ethical and is decidedly prescriptive. The issue of laughter is the issue of its acceptability. Laughter can be enlisted in a cause to the degree that it sanitizes its employment of the forbidden (the offensive). It is in fact management of the offensive that is its rhetorical function: make the jury laugh without alarming their sensibilities.

Central as the art of swaying an assembly or winning over a jury was to public life in antiquity—and Quintilian lines up a parcel of bons mots that carried the day in their time—it is comedy that principally calls up reflection on the nature (by way of the function) of the risible.

Citing Cicero, Donatus launched what was to be one of the major commonplaces regarding the nature of comedy: "Comedy is an imitation of life, a mirror of custom, an image of truth" (1:22). Oddly enough, this triple evocation of mimesis which sets out a program of fidelity to experience makes no special place for either the risible or the ludicrous. It is as if it was taken for granted that an accurate representation of ordinary life gives grounds for amusement. That, in fact, is the tongue-in-cheek inference drawn by Fielding in his preface to *Joseph Andrews*: "And perhaps there is one reason why a comic writer should of all others be the least excused for deviating from nature, since it may not be always so easy for a serious poet to meet with the great and the admirable; but life everywhere furnishes an accurate observer with the ridiculous" (12). Molière before him had drawn from the same observation a more self-serving conclusion. The obligation laid on the comic poet to furnish an accurate representation of recognizable types showed his art beset with greater difficulty than that of the tragic poet. To amuse without concession to lewdness and vulgarity was a heavy task: "C'est une étrange entreprise que celle de faire rire les honnêtes gens [It is no easy matter to make the better sort laugh]" (*Théâtre* 1:503).

But perhaps the assignment of representing human affairs in the unadorned style of everyday life, the *sermo hu-*

milis of Terence and Plautus, derived originally from the class distinction implicit in Aristotle's antithesis: "characters of a lower type" in comedy (5.1), "higher types of character" in epic and tragedy (3.2). Once the truculent men in the street—sausage sellers and the like—portrayed by Aristophanes had given way to Menander's scenes from the middle class, the image of "low" pretty much began to coincide with merely unheroic reality and comedy extended its purview to the bloodless crises of quotidian existence. Pierre Corneille, in 1660, was to make the point that the unheroic could pertain to the love affairs of the socially and politically exalted: a prince in love was not automatically tragic, no more than a commoner was to be thought necessarily diverting on stage (1:66–69). Dr. Johnson settled the matter in frolicsome fashion: "They seem to have thought," he wrote of authors who took refuge in that way of seeing the matter,

> that as the meanness of personages constituted comedy, their greatness was sufficient to form a tragedy; and that nothing was necessary but that they should croud the scene with monarchs, and generals, and guards; and make them talk, at certain intervals, of the downfall of kingdoms, and the rout of armies. They have not considered, that thoughts or incidents in themselves ridiculous, grow still more grotesque by the solemnity of such characters. (4:301)

However broadly or narrowly defined, the first postulate regarding the comic launched by Aristotle's dictum firmly anchored comedy to the representation of social existence as it falls below the norm set by magnates and grandees, whose downfall was imbued (in their own eyes) with epic or tragic reverberations.

The second assumption is closely linked to the first. "Comedia castigat ridendo mores [Comedy redresses manners laughingly]" runs the crisp summation of that view given by the seventeenth-century Neo-Latin poet Jean de Santeul. The ludicrous, being a subspecies of the ugly, marks a violation of the norm, a fault that calls down upon itself the (relatively) mild castigation of laughter.[1] The utilitarian view was to prevail pretty much as long as the theater itself felt in need of justification—roughly until the Romantic movement sanctified the role of the artist. While it held sway, the moralizing function of laughter completed the two-step vindication of comedy by way of its authorized definition: a faithful representation of prevailing manners that acted as an efficacious reproof, as a lively and convincing critique. Laughter was thus enlisted on the side of the angels. As Dryden was to put it, "the shame of that laughter, teaches us to amend what is ridiculous in our manners" (209).

The "realism" of comedy, in this view, the injunction that it mirror nature, thus stood hostage to its moralizing function. To the degree that we recognized ourselves in the portrayal, we were apt to mend our ways. The praise of Menander so extravagantly sounded by Aristophanes of Byzantium came on grounds of trompe l'oeil fidelity to human nature: "O Menander and Life, which of you imitated the other?" (cited by D. M. Halperin 241). Terence in his turn garnered highest esteem for his lifelike portrayals. Molière's contemporaries, both friend and foe, held it as an article of faith that he picked his victims off notebook in hand (see Théâtre 1:529). Thus a whole critical tradition cheerfully blinded itself to the presence in comedy of so much that is fantastic or illogical. It did so in the fervent expectation that laughter had the capacity to purge us of our ridicules, given a lifelike rendition.

---

[1] Hamartema, rendered by W. H. Fyfe as "blunder," is closely related to hamartia, the celebrated tragic flaw. For Santeul's motto, see Petit Larousse dictionary, pink pages.

The Aristotelian inheritance—some might say incubus—though no longer a predominant outlook can still be
glimpsed in an oddly unworldly salute to the supposed
powers of comedy from the post-Kantian pen of August
Wilhelm von Schlegel:

> Whoever has no knowledge of the world is perpetually in
> danger of making a wrong application of moral principles to
> individual cases, and, so with the very best of intentions in the
> world, may occasion much mischief to himself and others.
> Comedy is intended to sharpen our powers of discrimination,
> both of persons and situations; to make us shrewder; and this
> is its true and only possible morality. (187)

Art as handmaiden to philosophy is called upon to retranslate the pronouncements of the latter into the language
of praxis, of which it is still the recognized transcription.
Moral utility here descends to an almost ludicrous level of
utilitarian application. Comedy is made into the *vade mecum*
of the otherwise sadly perplexed metaphysician. To the
practicing Kantian, after all, a lie to save another's life is
inadmissible. When the Gestapo knocks at your door you
cannot but admit that a Jew lies hidden in the attic. A dash
of comic savoir faire may not be out of place in the land of
the categorical.

One is reminded of the mirror-image application which,
in *Rameau's Nephew,* the raffish François Rameau made into
the cornerstone of his own reading practice: "When I read
The Miser, I say to myself: 'Be as miserly as you like but
don't talk like the miser.' When I read *Tartuffe,* I say: 'Be a
hypocrite if you choose, but don't talk like one. Keep any
useful vices, but don't acquire the tone and art that would
make you ridiculous'" (Diderot 50). Whether high- or low-
minded, the fundamental outlook remains the same: comedy serves up the spectacle of the world's skullduggery—

avoid the pitfalls, be not yourself laughable. Expertise appears as the end product of that line of thinking about the risible: the expertise of the moralist shorn of his previous naivete, the expertise of the immoralist taught the value of taking cover.

A curious end-of-the-line summation of the laughter-moralized point of view reemerges at the end of the nineteenth century in the flowery prose of George Meredith's *Essay on Comedy* of 1877:

> Whenever they wax out of proportion, overblown, affected, pretentious, bombastical, hypocritical, pedantic, fantastically delicate, whenever it sees them self-deceived or hoodwinked, given to run riot in idolatries, drifting into vanities, congregating in absurdities, planning shortsightedly, plotting dementedly; whenever they are at variance with their professions . . . ; whenever they offend sound reason, fair justice; are false in humility or mined with conceit . . . —the Spirit overhead will look humanely malign and cast an oblique light on them, followed by volleys of silvery laughter. That is the Comic Spirit. (83–84)

Rude guffaws, I fear, are more apt to greet the mincing exuberance of this tribute than silvery laughter, but with due allowance for the changeability of fashion, the statement does no more than wrap in Victorian tinsel the functional view of laughter. The cudgel of old-fashioned comedy has merely been asked to make way for the fairy wand of the Comic Spirit, in deference to the diminished forthrightness of the age.

Henri Bergson, on the other hand, who opens up the twentieth century with an essay squarely entitled *Le rire* (Laughter), takes, in plainest terms, the functional-utilitarian view of laughter to its most uncompromising whistle-blowing conclusion:

We laugh every time a person gives us the impression of being a thing. . . . The comic is that side of a person which reveals his likeness to a thing, that aspect of human events which, through its peculiar inelasticity, conveys the impression of pure mechanism, of automatism, of movement without life. Consequently it expresses an individual or collective imperfection which calls for an immediate corrective. The corrective is laughter, a social gesture that singles out and represses a special kind of absentmindedness in men and events. (97, 117)

The cat, one is tempted to say, is out of the bag. Aristotle's unthreatening distortion, of the order of a comic mask, called forth no more than laughter, being adjudged insignificant. No harm done, none intended in return—the whole matter dismissed to attend to tragedy. Still, for all that it was seen as a mild reaction to an inconsequential blemish, laughter was a check, a rebuke of sorts. Later commentators amplified that role. Let Bergson now read the comic as a failure of conformity to our organic being, a mechanical rigidity fastened upon the fluidity of live motion, *du mécanique plaqué sur du vivant,* and laughter springs up in its corrective, its repressive guise, to bring the errant member into step with the rest of us. The fellow who shows up in a brown suit at a white tie dinner is swiftly and bloodlessly cured of an absentmindedness that threatens the good order of the body social. No more nakedly forthright a leap to the police function of laughter could be imagined; nor, given the notoriously irrepressible character of that reflex, could a more unlikely candidate for that function be trotted up. Certainly one of the issues raised by the functional that has to be tackled before we are finished with it is motive. What could impel one to want to assign to laughter a function so at variance with the explosive spontaneity of its common occurrences, the protean variability of the occasions for it? Why, in fact, seek to attribute to it a function in the first place?

An answer to the latter question arises with the birth of that late nineteenth-century creation, sociology. The age of science, of social science more particularly, was to set the question of the function of laughter on an axiomatic basis. "Le problème sociologique du rire," wrote Ernest Dupréel in an essay by that title, "c'est tout le problème du rire [The sociological problem of laughter is the whole of the problem of laughter]" (213). The pat assertion leads to a split-up. Laughter falls into two types, in the main: laughter of welcome (*le rire d'accueil*), laughter of rejection (*le rire d'exclusion*). The former cements union, seals a tacit compact, creates and celebrates the kind of unison on which group life thrives. The latter sets up a border, erects the wall of exclusion that defines the group by the counterexample of who does not belong. Dupréel generously opts for the predominance of the former over the latter, but clearly the laughter of exclusion forges as powerful a bond in the clique that is doing the laughing at another's expense (albeit momentary) as ever the laughter of welcome could— sinners that we are.

Jean Fourastié accurately names the encompassing mood to which the laughter that sets one at ease belongs: conviviality (66). A distinguished economist, Fourastié is able to seize upon the pervasiveness of laughter, unblinkered by the specialist's concern with it as primarily an aesthetic phenomenon. Laughter, he reminds us, resounds all around us at all hours of the day—on the street, in the workplace, at a meal or especially a banquet, in the parlor or the bedchamber. Chuckles, giggles, cackles, and guffaws are the unheard background noise of one's daily round— near or far from us; so much so that the solemnity of places or occasions where laughter is not to be heard stands out in our experience, earning itself a special recognition. Much of that laughter is no more than the ebullience of one's high spirits, much of it also born of a wish to counteract what would otherwise depress our spirits. Practically all of it arises from the social scene, the copresence of fellow human beings whose intercourse is leavened with constant reassurance, by way of laughter, that all is well, all is safe.

The case scarcely needs to be made for laughter and smiling as the universal lubricants of social intercourse. Jacob Levine makes it *a contrario* when he speaks of "these early depressed states where the infants cannot learn to use smiling or laughing as so-called 'social releasers' to evoke positive responses from others" (129). As the French saying has it, laughter disarms. Defenses are lowered, wrath is turned away as with a kind word, geniality—audibly— prevails. There is no underestimating the monumental task of daily pacification thus daily and ubiquitously performed. W. H. Martineau, citing H. G. Pitchford, describes inoffensive humor as the "universal shortcuts to consensus" (116). Sociology would indeed be remiss if it did not lay claim to an understanding of laughter in its own terms, those that class all human phenomena by the parts they play in social existence.

The place of laughter in the economy of small groups, on the other hand, brings into focus the small grain of social experience, its actual workings in specific circumstances. Social existence, for most of us, is a matter of fitting ourselves into a finite set of small groupings—be it the family, the workplace, the club, or the beach party. Laughter figures in variegated ways in the constant adjustments required for the smooth functioning of these social organisms. The exclusionary function noted by Dupréel here comes into its own in such mild hazing tactics as the so-called hotfoot whereby the new recruit, the greenhorn, pays the dues of integration into an army unit, let us say. As a rite of passage, the practical joke first compensates the collectivity for the mild disarray into which it is thrown by a new arrival, paying themselves out with laughter at the stranger's expense. The newcomer, for her own part, earns

membership at the cost of a passing discomfort greeted
with an uproarious mirth in which it were best to join in,
proving oneself of proper mettle and in the same motion
overleaping the barrier of estrangement. Bergson, as it happens, calls laughter *une brimade,* which pretty exactly translates as hazing.

The joke itself, in its capacity as a creator of ephemeral
unison, binds a group of listeners together as a unit of
the like-minded who join in a loud confirmatory chorus to
signal the sharing of a sudden understanding. It offers as
such a threat of potential rejection. In his study of the dirty
joke as a mode of transmissibility of privileged (in this case
sexual) information among the young, Harvey Sacks makes
the point that "since failing to 'get' the joke can be treated as, e.g., a sign of one's lack of sophistication, then the
social circumstances . . . urge a recipient to be working to
find what the punch line means. And from the joke's beginning that will be the test of him" (259). We have all
known the tenseness of an anticipated punch line, the mild
anxiety that a failure to join in would brand us an instant
outsider to the company of the mirthful. Having to have
the joke explained to one is certainly one of the less glorious moments of one's social existence. It is, moreover, a
clear case of double jeopardy, as we find ourselves missing out on the joy of unison as well as on the laughter itself (which no joke "explained" can revive; see Eastman
chap. 1).

As an irrefutable sign of unpremeditated unison, laughter is as much test of group belonging as it is formative
of such at-oneness. Lucie Olbrechts-Tyteca puts it well:
"Laughter is a way of testifying to the fact that one knows
what one has to know to belong to the group" (396). So far
from being adventitious, the mild explosion that punctu-
ates social intercourse at that astounding rate earlier cited
of 150 occurrences an hour is to be reckoned a foundational

ingredient in the ability of humans to put up with one another, in the changing kaleidoscope of groupings of which society consists. What has been termed the homeostasis of group existence is ensured by the constant definition and redefinition of the shared norms that constitute group identity. Dieter Wellershoff—to revert to the joke—sums it up incisively: "It functions as a test. The group verifies thereby the threshold of acceptable norm violation, its reactions to the transgressive, the functioning of its alarm mechanism: laughter, in a word" (336). The joke that falls flat, on this showing, gives as good a measure of how far the group will go in its defiance of more generally established pieties as the joke that goes over. What is at stake in either is the standing of the risk-taking individual who tells it. The rewards pretty much balance the occasional loss. Telling a joke that convulses your peers is a sweet experience, for laughter is a kind of loving, the grateful embrace of those it has released from the obligation to—as the injunction has it—"carry on." To give it Jean Guillaumin's Freudian translation: "To shine by one's wit or to make others laugh is to conciliate those 'others' by a complicity which forbids them to become your judge, it is to seduce the superego" (643). The converse is only too bitterly true, as the utterer of a failed bon mot can readily testify.

Parenthetically, the phenomenon known in French as *le fou rire*, an attack of the giggles, which as we have seen has also been known to take on epidemic and pathological proportions, provides an excellent paradigm of laughter's power to promote ephemeral unison by way of disruption. *Fou rire* presents unalloyed the almost instant contagiousness of laughter. It is enough to look into the eye of a friend or an acquaintance or even a stranger giving off the merest inkling that a syllable in the speaker's drone has

been construed subversively to find the shared consciousness of that innocent subversion an irresistible call to hilarity, the more overpowering as the occasion enjoins gravity.
Laughter thus picks out the like-minded, knitting them into
an instant fellowship born in part of the wish to disrupt the
larger assemblage. Communion there is, in cases of this
nature, but it is a communion in the inadmissible—laughter at a funeral, giggles in the church pew. I return to the
double-edged nature of the phenomenon in my recapitula-
tion, for a lesson lurks in that faculty of creating unison at
the cost of impending chaos.

That the reverse is also true, that laughter may be
quenched or seriously inhibited by the demeanor of the
unlaughing, has been quantifiably verified. In an experiment already alluded to, Kate Osborne and Antony Chapman measured a considerable variation in the amount and
duration of laughter occasioned, under controlled conditions, by funny material when viewed accompanied by an
unresponsive companion, alone, or with a responsive companion. On a scale of 0 to 140, frequency went from less
than 10 to 80 to 130; duration, on a scale of 0 to 180, went
from under 10 to 110 to 170. Whatever we may think of
quantification in these matters, these figures speak to one's
own experience: they are not, shall I say, counterintuitive.
Viewed either as fostering at least temporary concord, or
withering in its absence, dying on one's lips under a sober
or a forbidding gaze, laughter can be unhesitatingly referred to the sociable dimension of our being.

On this issue, a final observation. Consider the difficulty
of laughing alone at a set of others who, either vexed or
simply unamused, do not join in. It is the very definition of
what is called a hollow laugh—mirthless, and soon to die
of its own accord.

There remains to situate laughter in its anthropological

dimension, to see what can be learned by viewing it in the optic of the considerable, the mind-boggling dissimilarity of cultural contexts.

W. W. Pilcher's study of a so-called subculture, *The Portland Longshoremen*, gives us what we might call a micro-ethnographic view, taking a professional milieu as an entity, complete with ritual and mythology, acting as a distinct variant within the larger culture. "Joking behavior," Pilcher reports, "controls real aggressive and antagonistic feelings so that a stable system of social behavior may be maintained through group solidarity" (112). In the rough and tumble of an arduous occupation where bodily harm is not an out-of-the-way possibility, the need to "let off steam" is more than evident. Ritualized insult operates as jocosely filtered aggression, couched in the language and the occasions of that particular line of work. Comparable behavior, in accents less forceful and terms borrowed from another occupation, is brought out in a study of a London department store.[2] Drawn from environments both far-flung and distinct within the same larger ambient culture, these joking behaviors exhibit both a sameness (fundamental) and a difference (superficial) that easily bring home the lesson of a stabilizing, homeostatic function across widely separated strata.

A celebrated essay by A. R. Radcliffe-Brown, "On Joking Relationships," gives that same point considerable extension. First, a definition: "What is meant by the term 'joking relationship' is a relation between two persons in which one is by custom permitted, and in some instances required, to tease or make fun of the other, who in turn is required to take no offense . . . not only in Africa but also in Asia, Oceania and North America" (195).

---

[2] Pamela Bradney, "The Joking Relationship in Industry," *Human Relations* 10 (1957): 179–87.

A relation, as the author terms it, "of permitted disrespect" (196), the joking relationship appears to hinge, in his analysis, on the copresence of attachment and separation, conjunction and disjunction, as in the in-law relationship. A "playful antagonism" expresses both sides of this conjunction of opposites: the hostility evoked by the outsider, "the friendliness that takes no offense at insult" (197–98). Grandparents and grandchildren traditionally celebrate their closeness allied with generational distance by ritualized teasing that often takes the form for the one (grandfather or grandchild) to pretend to wish to, or to be, married to the other's wife (202). The teasing may get a little rough, and Mahadev Apte reports, amusingly enough, that "in some instances, the unwilling and aggrieved parties took matters to court" only to be reminded that they "belonged to the specific kinship category with which [the defendants] were privileged to have a joking relationship" (17). Thus, though the release of aggression in word and deed might well at times be felt to pass the limits of playfulness, the spirit of laughter is known to preside over a whole category of mutual behaviors, enjoining, as it were, amusement where anger might otherwise not be out of place. The parallel with the tolerance enjoyed by the practical joker, in the schoolyard or in the barracks, is hard to escape. In his case also a taboo on open resentment operates, for it brands one a "bad sport," unable to hold his own with equanimity in the ebullience of a certain kind of social existence.

Whether we envisage the question sociologically, that is, in terms of the management of tensions that inhere in the structures of social existence, wherever and at whatever degree of complexity it presents itself, or anthropologically, looking at the specific structures that characterize specific cultural arrangements spanning time and place on this terraqueous globe, it should be pretty clear by now that laughter is called upon to disrupt an order, briefly and reversibly, in the interest of a more viable continuation of that order. Aggression is vented, so to speak, in the interests of nonaggression.

The answer thus jointly returned by the social sciences, at such times as they take cognizance of laughter altogether, is by way of assigning to it a function in the economy of collective existence. A prior question may now be asked: what is the intellectual warrant for such a functional approach? on what principle do we seek an understanding of laughter by an integrative move that finds a place for it in the process of human adaptation to the demands of social existence. *Process, adaptation:* our vocabulary as much as gives the game away—it is the Darwinian imperative that shapes out thinking in this realm. We must look to biology for our master plan.

In its broadest outline the Darwinian postulate of natural selection authorizes the explanatory method that is operative in the social sciences. As the end result of a process of selection founded on the superior adaptation of the organisms that survived, evolution presupposes that all that *did* survive, *had* to. Having "evolved" to this day, they represent the sum of those superior adaptations that allowed them to thrive where others, no longer to be seen on God's green earth, went under. In a somewhat crass revision of Pope's "whatever is, is right," the Darwinian hypothesis leads one to a mode of understanding that takes the updated form "whatever is, is functional." Any feature of our present animate landscape, in other words, can be said to be understood only when its role in the survival of whatever entity it helps to constitute has been satisfactorily assigned. Let the human animal be said to be the animal that laughs; then laughter, to be understood, must be integrated into an account of the success of that species in resisting elimination. Laughter, in other words, must be shown to have survival value.

Specifically, Darwinian speculation has in recent decades fastened on the appeasement display as both evolutionary outcome and functional explanation of the place of laughter in the human adaptive progress. J. A. R. A. M. van Hooff traces the ancestry of human laughter to something like the "relaxed open-mouthed display in chimpanzees," having first established that "in the ascending scale of the primates leading to man, there is a progressive broadening of the meaning of the element of baring the teeth. Originally forming part of a mainly defensive or protective pattern of behaviour, this element becomes a signal of submission and non-hostility" (217). Elsewhere we read a more pin-pointed placement of the phenomenon (or rather of its explanation):

> Bolwig . . . considers the play-face to be a development of the ritualized play-bite in which the lips are drawn tightly over the teeth, thus effectively covering them. Smiling in humans is seen as a further step in the ritualizing of the play-bite; and the fact that both rows of teeth are often exposed further suggests the element of appeasement since it now resembles the sub-human primate's fear-grin more closely than it does the play-face. The soft guttural staccato exhalations that often accompany the play-face are seen by Bolwig to be the origin of laughter. (Loizos 205)

There is something ironic in an explanatory mode that simultaneously robs humankind of its monopoly of mirthful laughter and endows that apparently gratuitous outburst with awesome powers fit to ensure our preservation as a species. The matter is summed up thus by W. F. Fry, Jr.: "Laughter's appeasement display obviates violent competition sparing individuals. And it also enhances opportunity for the cooperative gregarious behaviour which is responsible for so much human productivity and which is one of man's greatest biological assets" (25).

Though mirthful laughter and the faculty of amusement it presupposes precisely beg the question of such a narrow-gauge accounting for its existence, there is undeniably a peacemaking function (*le rire désarme*, laughter disarms) that must be associated with our ability to "laugh off" our differences; and without necessarily granting explanatory priority to a functional stance, it must be given its place in any comprehensive account of a phenomenon characterized at once by its apparent marginality and its insistent audibility.

Emblematic of that marginality, equally insistent in his ubiquity, the Fool boasts a genealogy that stretches back to mythological times and forward to the stand-up comic, his latest avatar. From the native American Trickster to Renaissance court jester, from eighteenth-century German university professor to borscht circuit entertainer, from the medieval Confrérie de la Basoche to the Barnum and Bailey circus clown, Folly, whose self-praise was penned by the learned quill of Desiderius Erasmus, stands guard over the realm of the risible. She stumbles, and we laugh. Her servants at one time wore motley, emblem of breakdown, before donning Chaplin's outsized shoes and diminutive bowler hat. They brandished a bauble, both phallic and testicular, with which to goose the bystanders. To this day they sport under nomad canvas the ill-fitting clothes, the white paint mask, the red nose that mark them as otherworldly apparitions, reassuringly inept, and for all that more than a little untrustworthy.

The Trickster of Winnebago legend is a figure of folly in its twin guises of ineptitude and mischief making. He cohabits with women before a war party, breaking a taboo and therefore aborting the party. His right arm engages the left arm in combat. He brands his own anus for failing to wake him as the foxes steal his meat. He sends his penis across the water to rape the chief's daughter. He kills the children whose mothers he has sent off in search of plums, promising to guard their young; instead he boils and eats them. He rashly chews a bulb that warned that he who chews it will defecate: soon he breaks wind with such force as to uproot the trees to which he clings, then nearly drowns in the sea of his own excrement. The victim of his own rashness, of his credulity, of his totally uncurbed appetites, of his ill-placed self-confidence, he misses no chance to victimize others with a gratuitous viciousness that mingles with bland equanimity. He is an object lesson in the perilousness of folly, to itself and to others. Karl Kerényi, in the postscript of Paul Radin's classic study, *The Trickster: A Study in American Indian Mythology*, comments that "Trickster is . . . exhibiting his true nature as—so we can sum up, under a single active principle, the component elements 'phallic', 'voracious', 'sly', 'stupid'—*the spirit of disorder, the enemy of boundaries*" (185).

Two significant and not unrelated aspects of the fool, one probably derived from the other, stand disclosed in the person of the Trickster. In *Pretend the World Is Funny and Forever*, Seymour and Rhoda Fisher characterize the fool as "a form of tamed chaos" (51). The enemy of boundaries stands guard over the bounded universe of a culture, looks beyond it to what lurks out there, unabsorbed and unabsorbable, the threatening figure of all the culture stands against, of all it fears, the taboo—and it cheerfully takes it on, incorporates it, reduces it to a figure of incoherence, of motley, fit to raise gales of laughter. Laura Makarius gives a convincing account of the nature and ultimate import of this performance: "Among the Navaho . . . the Natani . . . treat their patients by . . . rocking them in a blanket. 'They had . . . a small piece of sheepskin with a red blotch in the centre. . . . the blood on the sheepskin must be something disgusting and powerful. It may be the excretion of the sore of a horse, or menstrual fluid. A man shows his power by not fearing it' " (49). Swallowing the contents of buckets of urine "with relish" (48–49), handling that object of fearsome revulsion, menstrual blood, the clowns skate with enviable ease over the unthinkable by wallowing in the unmentionable. The culture's unspoken anxieties are rehearsed, made manageable in the laughable exhibition. The "violation of taboo is their *raison d'être*," writes Makarius of these clowns (53); but did I not read somewhere the answer given by a native informant to the visiting ethnologist's question, How is taboo violation dealt with?—with laughter.

Guardian of the cosmic order by the casual ingestion of the untouchable, the clown stands heir to the other side of the Trickster's being, his supernatural character.

Trickster's godlike nature is as problematic, as tricky, we might say, as is his nature altogether. Paul Radin puts it thus: "The overwhelming majority of all so-called trickster myths in North America give an account of the creation of the earth, or at least the transforming of the world, and have a hero who is always wandering, who is always hungry, who is not guided by normal conceptions of good and evil, who is either playing tricks on people or having them played on him and who is highly sexed. Almost everywhere he has some divine traits" (155). The integration of the spirit of disorder into the divine pantheon is perhaps a necessity, but it goes without saying that it throws the more responsible creator god, in particular, into something of a quandary: how to cope with this demolition expert, this sower of dissension and perturbation?

Kerényi looks back longingly to Hermes, the trickster of classical antiquity, whose powers of perturbation are not so out-of-hand as his American counterpart's. A glance at Trickster's career in Oglala myth, on the other hand, yields Radin a different insight:

> In a myth he himself states who he is: "I am a god and the son of a god. My father, the Rock, is the oldest of the gods. It is he

that named all things and made all languages that are spoken.
I have done much good and should be treated as a god, but
because my other parent, the Winged God, had no shape, my
form is queer and all laughed at me. When I do good all laugh
at me as if I were making sport, and since everyone laughs at
me I will laugh at them." (165)

Laughed at and laughing in return, Trickster thus embodies the spirit of laughter in both its repressive and its
expressive character, enthroning it very close to the center
of existence, the primal Rock on which creation reposes.
This recognition that the fool encompasses both the unacceptable and the holy—or that he represents the holy in
its unacceptable guise and is thence himself hallowed—
finds an echo in the sacred clowns already spoken of, as
well perhaps as in the leaping antics of dervish, shaman,
and even unshorn biblical prophet. Shakespeare's naturals,
licensed to speak their minds in deference to a simplicity
that gives their utterance the force of nature's own, are a
late semi-Christianized pagan remnant of that acceptance.[3]
Trickster, clown, natural thus all preserve order by offering
disorder safe harbor within its precincts. Homeostasis is
served in the large as it had been the function of laughter
to serve it in the gatherings of the few.

Finally, the medieval church's Feast of Fools, its Feast of
Asses, its Holy Innocents' Day represent the incursion of
the comic in holy scandals at the heart of a cult that, to all

---

[3] Harlequin, it must be added, is said to have appeared first "in history
or legend as an aerial spectre or demon [Hellequin], leading that ghostly
nocturnal cortège known as the Wild Hunt ['la maisnie Herlechin']," but,
"as time went on . . . the wailing procession of lost souls turned into a
troop of comic demons" (Welsford 287–88). The devils of the mystery plays
also ended up playing the fools, so much so that the demise of the genre
was brought about by its prohibition by the civil authorities when the
pranks got out of hand.

appearances, repudiates laughter. M. C. Hyers gives the
following account of such goings on:

> On Holy Innocents' Day (*festum puerorum*), the gravity and
> grandeur of the holy office of bishop was suspended in the
> appointment of a boy bishop. For a day the awesome authority
> and responsibility of the church was returned to the playful
> innocence of childhood, with the boy bishop officiating at a
> service in which the ecclesiastical positions and functions were
> assumed by children. . . . The Feast of Fools (*festum stultorum*)
> had less of the aura of innocence about it. In a period of
> revelling following Christmas, the inferior clergy burlesqued
> the offices and roles of their superiors. In many cases a Lord of
> Misrule was elected to supplant the holder of the *baculus*
> (wand of office), his installation occurring at Vespers during
> that portion of the *Magnificat* beginning with the words, "He
> hath put down the mighty from their seat, and exalted them of
> low degree (Luke 1:52). (18)

The common denominator of these enshrined festivals of
folly, whether or not it is placed under the authority of
a Lord of Misrule, is the proclamation of a holiday from
accepted authority, from life under rule. It is the inversion
of established hierarchies into the state of topsy-turvy. One
other such inversion is chronicled by Natalie Zemon Davis
under the programmatic title "Women on Top" (especially 129).

William Willeford traces the Feast of Fools to the Roman
Saturnalia (in which slaves were masters for a day, reinsti-
tuting the equality that was said to have obtained under
the rule of Saturn). He sees in them "probably survivals
from an even more ancient intercalary period inserted into
the calendar to fill the gap between solar and lunar year"
(69). In this time outside of time, lawfulness could be
suspended, misrule allowed to break in upon the world
briefly, chaos celebrated in relief from the oppressiveness of

order. As a release of (demonic?) energies pent up under
rule, folly had its day outside days, in which it could do
boisterous justice to all the culture perforce repressed, to
what Jung, in his postscript to Radin's book, termed its
"shadow" (202).

The lesson of folly thus meets up with that enunciated
by the sociologist: laughter preserves the equilibrium of a
culture as it does that of a group, by timely release of an
outburst that dissipates animosities. The unspoken resentment that Freud, in *Civilization and Its Discontents*, traces to
"instinctual renunciation" finds an outlet in a celebration
that briefly, and collectively, throws off the yoke of the
rational and institutional in an all-out version of today's
meek and pallid office party.

Is this then how the laughter evoked by folly in its mul-
tiple guises is to be assessed in the perspective of the
functional? A further observation may be in order. Keeping
in mind a capital observation of Apte's ("The functional
explanations proposed by anthropologists have only occasionally been acknowledged or accepted by members of the
cultures in which the joking relationships exist," 61), let us
consider an early remark of Radin's as he tried to assess the
significance of the laughter evoked among the American
Indians by the figure of Trickster: "It is difficult to say
whether the audience is laughing at him, at the tricks he
plays on others, or at the implications his behaviour and
activities have for them" (xxiv). Quite apart from the shaft
of blinding light this remark so casually throws on the
status of "scientific" explanation in this domain, the quandary it outlines is illuminating from the sharp relief into
which it throws the multifaceted figure of the Fool. Do we
laugh at him? do we laugh with him? do we, through him,
laugh at ourselves? An answer that strongly suggests itself
is that our laughter, at one time or another, partakes of all
three of these modes. Folly, then, which, in concert with

Erasmus, Montaigne took to be the figure of the human condition, in its amalgam of mischief and ineptitude, may well bring out laughter in the pure state: an unanalyzable reaction to *the way things are,* precipitated by an egregious representation of that sorry truth. The sum of our short-comings we cannot in the ordinary way take notice of, as we carry on soberly the business of our lives. It is left to the feast of fools to make annual acknowledgment of our fallibility in an outburst of high spirits that takes the sting out of it.

Mischief and ineptitude, these two dependable laughing companions, hold the key to a significant countercurrent that must be given its place in the study of laughter, name-ly, the reprobation in which it is held by thinkers as diverse as Plato and Shelley, Bossuet and Baudelaire, Lord Chester-field and the abbé Lamennais. Laughter has its enemies, and it may be instructive to let them have their say, the more so since the grounds for their aversion may yield to us a deeper understanding of the functionalist position.

In the *Philebus* (47–50), Plato has Socrates advance the view that we laugh at the foolish conceit of those who think themselves wealthier, more handsome, but especially wiser than in fact they are. That conceit of theirs is harm-less, to us, for "those of them who have this false conceit and are weak and unable to revenge themselves when they are laughed at you may truly call ridiculous, but those who are strong and able to revenge themselves you will define most correctly . . . by calling them . . . hateful, for igno-rance in the powerful is hateful and infamous" (49C). The pleasure we take in the ignorance of others is a species of envy (pleasure in another's downfall). That we can experi-ence it only at the expense of those who threaten us no harm does not add to the moral coloration of that tainted joy. Viewed thus in a strictly moral perspective, laughter comes off as a faintly reprehensible pleasure, ill suited to

the company of the truly wise, those Houyhnhnms who
rejoice (soberly) only in the good.

That laughter should fare no better in the orthodox
Christian view is an unsurprising announcement. Bishop
Bossuet, in his *Maximes sur la comédie,* a 1694 broadside
against a hapless priest in his diocese who had the temerity
to approve of comedy, made it thunderingly plain.

I know of none among the ancient [fathers] who, far from
looking on jesting as an act of virtue, did not think of it as
vicious, though not invariably criminal or damnable. The least
harm they find in it is its uselessness, which enters it in the
ranks of that *idle talk* about which Jesus Christ teaches us that
we shall have to render an account on Judgment Day . . .

. . . Saint Paul, after taking the jest under its fairest guise
and naming it by its fairest name, ranks it among the
vices . . .

. . . Saint Ambrose, having recalled the words of Our Lord,
Woe unto you that laugh, marvels that Christians could "seek
occasions to laugh" . . .

. . . The Fathers tended to take literally those words of Our
Lord: *Woe unto you that laugh now! for you shall mourn and weep.*
Saint Basil, who concluded therefrom that it was not licit to
laugh "in any matter, if only on account of those who offend
God by despising his law," tempers this saying by the following in Ecclesiasticus: "A fool raises his voice in laughter, but a
prudent man at the most smiles gently." In conformity with
that saying he allows us, with Solomon, "to light up the
countenance a little with a modest smile." But as to those
"great outbursts and bodily upheavals" which are akin to
convulsion, they do not, according to him, belong to a man
"virtuous and self-possessed." (37:601–2, 605, 609)

The prohibition on laughter proper in favor of the more
restrained smile meets up, interestingly enough, with Lord
Chesterfield's self-portrayal in this regard. Christian stern-

ness thus falls in unexpectedly with patrician gravity: "I am neither of a melancholy, nor a cynical disposition; and am as willing, and as apt, to be pleased as anybody; but I am sure that, since I have had the full use of my reason, nobody has ever heard me laugh" (1:322). It may be noted that the Duke of La Rochefoucauld made a similar, though less absolute, declaration.

The enemies of laughter are not all drawn from the ranks of the guardians of conformity with reason, Christian compunction, or stoic composure. The poet Shelley, libertarian that he was, on one occasion avowed himself convinced "that there can be no entire regeneration of mankind until laughter is put down" (cited by J. R. Caldwell 252). A fellow poet of quite another stamp, Charles Baudelaire, in his "De l'essence du rire" (On the Essence of Laughter), saw laughter in a super-Hobbesian light, as coming "of the idea of one's superiority. A satanic idea, if there ever was one!" (376–77). Laughter, born of the Fall, is unthinkable in Paradise, where all things were created good: it was given us as an alleviation of a deplorable condition, of which it is a sign, no less so than tears. Imagine, he goes on, that pure-hearted heroine of *Paul et Virginie,* raised in an idyllic tropical island; imagine her come to Paris and faced with a caricature: she would not understand but surely she would recoil!

An even more intemperate condemnation flows from the pen of the abbé Lamennais, firebrand advocate of nineteenth-century liberal Catholicism, as far removed from Bossuet's staunch orthodoxy as could be imagined:

Laughter ever implies a motion in the direction of the self and ending up in the self, from the dreadful laughter of bitter irony, the frightful laughter of despair, the laughter of Satan, defeated and still resisting, hardening himself in unbendable pride, down to the degraded laughter of idiot or madman, or to that which is sparked by an unexpected naivete, a silly

blunder, a bizarre mismatch. Never does it lend the countenance an air of sympathy or good will. Quite the opposite, it
causes the most harmonious visage to grimace, it expunges
beauty. It is one of the faces of evil: not that it expresses it
outright, but it points to the seat of evil. (247)

Romanticism is writ large in these latter protestations.
Idealistic philosophy, Christianity as a religion that saw in
the torment of the Cross the answer to the sinfulness of
humankind, the Stoics with their injunction to be above it
all (*nil admirari*) all had their reasons to put laughter down.
Romanticism was able in its turn to take a view of the
human condition that consigned laughter to the hellish
glow of the eternally unreconciled, the cynically disabused.
Light-minded mirth was lost sight of as even a possibility
in these divergent variants of a common repudiation.

For all that it strikes us as wrongheaded and deter-
minedly one-sided in its confinement of laughter to its own
worst-case scenario, in malice and caricature, heedlessness
and profane violence, the repudiation of laughter has a
lesson to teach us with regard to the comic. What Plato and
Bossuet and Baudelaire are led to dispraise in laughter is
the undeniable charge of aggressiveness that is practically
inseparable from its occurrence. I try to come to grips in
the next chapter with the Hobbesian view that makes such
aggression the be-all of laughter. Short of that kind of simplification, the anarchic potential of an outburst that is apt
to occur in any context, under any circumstances, permissible or impermissible, is the more threatening to its would-
be targets as it is both irrefutable and unpredictable: laughter cannot be put down except by more laughter, and it
strikes where it pleases. The threat of uncontained disorder
can be readily measured by the anxiety it arouses in the
bosom of the firmly committed, be it to a Cause or to a
Value.

What then begins to make sense is the eagerness of the

proponents of laughter seen as the upholder of a norm, the servant of an order. It may be shortsighted to seek to reduce the stress on function to a wish to channel dangerous energies into a constructive role, but the suspicion exists that such an impulse is not foreign to this outlook. Laughter's disruptive character comports so ill with the policing function assigned to it by Bergson and Meredith that—even though it *does* fulfill it on occasion—the strong suggestion subsists that we are faced with a case of co-optation: the unprincipled thug enrolled in the police—*les forces de l'ordre*, to revert once again to a suggestive French phrase. *Castigat ridendo mores* would of course gain enormous persuasive force if it were possible to point to a single instance, in the history of comedy, of a miser, a seducer, a bully, a false prude, or a hypocrite shamed into the mending of his or her ways. The anonymous author of the *Letter on the Comedy of the Impostor*, thought by some to be Molière himself, adduced a remarkable argument in defense of *Tartuffe*. The ridicule cast on the palpable hypocrisy of the seduction scene would make women proof against the gilded speeches of future seducers by an irresistible recall of the conduct that had diverted them on the stage—ridicule being incompatible with persuasiveness. One wonders with how much of a straight face the argument was mounted, but a better case of logic clashing with fact could scarcely be devised.

What image of laughter, to sum it all up, do we carry forward from this line of investigation? The quest for a recognizable function, though fueled in part by the kind of anxiety exhibited by the anathemas laughter called upon its head, was by no means wholly negative. In the small grain of daily life and of small group intercourse—the family, the workplace, the discussion group, the club—laughter operates to ensure homeostasis by the ventilation of manageable hostility, the timely and short-lived disruption of authority. Group cohesion, reinforced by the audible and unpremeditated expression of shared norms, is further cemented by the spontaneous exclusion, for the span of a laugh, of the butt of the joke, who if he manages to laugh at himself, however, averts even temporary ostracism. In the broader setting of the state, the privileged standing of the court jester today devolves on the satirical journal, the roasting party, the stand-up comic in her political-aggressive mode. One is reminded of Mort Sahl's immortal jibe at the candidates in the Nixon-Kennedy presidential race of 1960: "One of them wants to buy the country, the other wants to sell it!" Latitude for the mordant expression of political dissatisfaction is the mark of a well-regulated state, unthreatened by nonviolent dissent. The fate of a satirical weekly such as France's *Le canard enchaîné* (The Shackled Duck [=canard]), often dragged into court, seldom convicted, ever irrepressible and formidably well informed, is paradigmatic. What government can afford to tackle a laughing adversary successfully? not in a nation, at any rate, that put forward the proposition that ridicule kills.

In the widest setting, finally, that of a culture, possessed of a style, of an integrated worldview, the role of the festival of folly, the holiday from sense originally endowed with divine sanction (Trickster cycle, Feast of Fools), living on today in the circus clown, the Marx Brothers antics, the Monty Python Flying Circus, preserves on the largest scale the privilege of nonsense in the pursuit of sense, the beneficial eruption of disorder in the creation and maintenance of a living order. If, in fact, we look for an antidote to the maudlin dithyramb to the Comic Spirit penned by Meredith in praise of its narrowly conformist labors, none better exists than the delineation of the comic spirit as supremely anarchic we find in Cedric Whitman's spirited *Aristophanes and the Comic Hero:*

a desperate small fellow, inexcusably declaring himself for a social savior; an utterly self-centered rogue of *poneria* [malice], representing a universal gesture of thumb-to-nose unto all the high and mighty; a coward who runs away from his enemies for the moment, and then dances on their graves with a godless cheer; a fast talker, a hoper-for-the-best and a believer-in-the-worst; a creature of infinite ambition, infinite responsiveness, and infinite appetite—the comic hero, as represented in Aristophanes, somehow makes up a figure of salvation, survival against odds; he is the self militant, and devil-take-the-means. (52)

Oddly enough, then, it is to the anarchic character of laughter that we end up looking for aid in maintaining whole our allegiance to an orderly existence. The Aristophanic scamp lightens for us the burden of a necessary conformity. Laughter may in a general way keep us in line, in the Bergsonian-Meredithian sense, and comedy may well proffer a mirror in which we seek not to have to recognize our manners. Far more to the point, though, is the breathing spell hilarity provides. It relieves us from the very real and unshakable constraints of daily living. It lavishes on us the chance, many times a day, to bond and rebond with our fellows in unholy communion. It holds at bay the demons we fear by the safe passage it allows a licit perturbation. Such service we must keep in mind as we come to restate the business of laughter our own way.

CHAPTER THREE

Laughter's Inner Springs:
The Psychological Approach

Lachen heisst: schadenfreu zu sein, aber mit gutem Gewissen. [To laugh means: to take joy in mischief, but with a good conscience.]
—Friedrich Nietzsche

Life is free play fundamentally and would like to be free play altogether.
—George Santayana

The view from the inside, which seeks to identify laughter through the motivation it imputes to it—the psychological viewpoint, in other words—has launched four loosely related families of explanations upon the world: the theories of superiority, degradation, liberation, and play. A consideration of each in turn occupies the pages of this chapter.

Plato's view of laughter in the *Philebus* as the expression of our pleasure in the ignorance of someone not powerful enough to strike fear in us lays the blame for laughter, at least inferentially, on a misplaced sense of superiority. But no one before Hobbes tied laughter so indisputably to our self-love, in a phrase that bears repeating, as the unforgettable, the ringing formulation of the most widespread and the most influential of the psychological explanations: laughter, he wrote, proceeds from a "sudden glory arising

from some sudden conception of some eminency in ourselves, by comparison with the infirmity of others, or with
our own formerly" (chap. 9:13). The last clause offers a
saving grace: the possibility of laughing at oneself, an
awareness that fallibility falls to our own lot as well, albeit
in the past tense.

This view, at all events, though it may be distasteful has
a lot going for it. The enemies of laughter we encountered
in the preceding chapter speak eloquently to its "satanic"
character, to its apparent roots in self-regard, to its aggressiveness. No one who has experienced laughter directed at himself can have escaped the sense of mortifica-
tion, of belittlement, it inflicts. Conversely, even the most
innocent laughter, the laughter at a child's earnest misap-
prehension, or at the old gent suddenly and unaccountably
seated on the sidewalk, having slipped on a banana peel
(the paradigmatic icon of comic theory), lets peep out a ray
of malice, a sliver of self-congratulation. Should the hapless
skater taking a spill happen to be an enemy of ours, our
mirth, though not primarily imputable to what Freud terms
the *Tendenz* (here, aggressive), will not be the fainter . . .

Explosive, anarchic, disruptive full-bellied laughter in its
ear-splitting guffaws can scarcely deny a connection with a
loud assertiveness that smacks of superiority. But does such
evidence suffice to proclaim superiority the be-all of that
laughter, its motive force and originary impulse? Hobbes
and his followers appear to want to have it so. D. H. Monro puts it mildly: "There can be no doubt that, all refine-
ments aside, misfortunes are funny, simply in themselves"
(50); and before we can rush in to qualify, he adduces the
far wilder claim of Stephen Leacock's that "the oldest and
most primitive form of laughter is the shout of triumph
with which the savage exulted over his fallen foe" (32).

Descartes, in *Les passions de l'âme* (Treatise on the Passions of the Soul), enters a very significant qualifier:

Derision, or Mockery, [he defines as] a kind of Joy mixed in with Hatred which comes of our perceiving some small misfortune in a person we think deserving of it. We feel Hatred for the misfortune and Joy to see it in someone who deserves it: And when that occurs in a manner unforeseen the shock of the Surprise causes one to burst out laughing. . . . But that misfortune must be small; for if it is great, one cannot believe that he who undergoes it deserves to, unless one be ill-natured indeed, or feel much Hatred for him. (art. 178, "De la moquerie")

Descartes's modification of Hobbes's unqualified gloating is of weight. A sense of fitness is the corrective that turns the perception of one's own advantage in another's failing into the kind of joy, albeit *schadenfreu*, that is experienced, in Nietzsche's phrase cited as epigraph to this chapter, *mit gutem Gewissen*. Conscience is placated by the deservedness of the ill turn played either by fate or by a nimble opponent. The fall is richly earned, and it is . . . a pratfall (literally, on one's posterior)—from no great height, that is. Aristotle's all-important qualifier, that the deformity be painless (like the comic mask), here comes into play. We laugh on condition the old gentleman who so abruptly sat on the ice hasn't broken his coccyx, does not grimace in pain—just as we laugh all the harder if the skater was showing off, or if he was in the act of cutting us off at the pass. Hostility is not a necessary condition, but it is a great help. The irreplaceable ingredient is the laugher's own security: we only laugh when we can afford to.

The match perceived by Descartes between check received and offense given, when it is exact, both eases the laugher's conscience and rejoices her intellect, thus making for hilarity unimpeded.[1] The painlessness postulated by

[1] Jerry Suls neatly corroborates this principle of equity when he observes that, in a joke presented under laboratory conditions, "when the

Aristotle likewise unburdens us to laugh without fear or guilt. Yet here we must take into account local conditions, down to variabilities of both mood and sensibility. Elizabethans could laugh with a good conscience at the baiting of a bear; animal rights had not been thought of, animal pain was without standing and hence without reality in their *mentalité*. My neighbor may scoff good- or ill-naturedly at what gives me pain, just as a callused hand easily withstands the heat a softer skin may find intolerable. I laugh today at what yesterday struck me as appalling. Mood, distance, circumstance; parochial, historical, cultural determinants all enter into the infinitely variable mix that ensures a level of sensibility appropriate to seize the funniness of an event unclouded by its shadow, by its sobering aura of pain (or merely annoyance).

One person's innocent diversion, we know, is another's sadistic exercise. "Consciousness raising," in fact, is the name we give to the gradual elimination of permissible targets of mockery. Ethnic jokes that flourished uninhibitedly into the first decades of our own century, in America, are unlikely to be offered for indiscriminate amusement today. The bigoted do laugh, but brand themselves as bigoted by their laughter. Mothers-in-law are no longer the fair game they once were, interest groups spring up left and right to assert the common humanity of those whom a trait or a practice heretofore read out of the laughing communion. Laughter at another's expense may seem thereby imperiled, a prospect too remote to be taken much to heart. What this general evolution does betoken is that laughter requires a momentary invulnerability—to fear, to shared pain—that is incompatible with full-fledged fellow feeling. When the latter exists, or it is deemed politic to

misfortune [visited on the joke character] was seen as overretaliation, rated funniness and resolution decreased" (52).

pretend it exists, laughter occurs only by express permission—as in self-directed ethnic humor.

What Hobbes, then, saw unabashedly as recognition of one's own *eminency* in some respect or other may be retranslated as that invulnerability that preserves the laugher from uncomfortable kinship with the laughee in respect to the *infirmity* laughed at, or even if it is shared, preserves him from taking it to heart, from seeing it as disabling. Laughter, after all, is not always at another's expense (as Hobbes seems to imply); but even when it is—and the "other" may be, as Hobbes recognizes, "ourselves formerly"—amusement proceeds from a perceived disparity. He who laughs is, for the moment, firm rather than infirm: firm enough to abandon himself to the helpless convulsions that shake his frame without endangering it; firm in the recognition that, shared or not, the perceived infirmity leaves him free to laugh at it; firm enough to face with equanimity the possible resentment of the one he laughs at.[2] It is possible to speak of a condition so Olympian as superiority, but it is hard to reconcile it with chest thumping over a fallen enemy, to see laughter, in Ludovici's telling phrase, as a "spiritualized snarl." To imagine that we laugh out of a mood of self-aggrandizement pure and simple is to paint human nature in colors derived solely from the aggressive side of it. It is to imagine it Hobbesian. Intellectual special pleading, as we earlier recognized, is one of the besetting sins of comic theory. Quite fortunately, in this case, it flies in the face so directly of our own self-perceived sense of mirth that it is left to preach quite exclusively to the converted.

Two observations in the psychological literature, one relating to infant behavior, the other to that of the growing child, shore up our sense that the gist of the superiority

---

[2] Recall Plato's reminder that we laugh at the weak, quail at the strong.

view may be found in the requirement of mastery, of effective control of the laughing matter. The first is from an essay by L. A. Sroufe, E. Water, and L. Matas:

> When any new or discrepant stimulus is first encountered, there is an initial orienting and appraisal process. Physiological records of arousal do not differ until after this appraisal has occurred. If the event is evaluated as safe or unthreatening, smiling or laughter will occur. If the child is insecure or interprets the event as a threat, crying or some other form of negative affect will occur.[3]

In the quasi-feral responsiveness of the infant, the unexpected is the potentially threatening. Funniness can be achieved by the reversal from threat to reassurance, a sudden approach that turns into emphatic nuzzling. Euphoria greets a pleasant surprise, disruption that wraps itself in an ambiance of positivity—a cooing, a nuzzle, a hug. Laughter erupts on the strength of renewed confidence that all, so far, is well with the world. Tears are not far off—the decision may hang by a hair, the "appraisal" is not wholly predictable: how much sudden motion is too much? Not having lost her footing, so to speak, the infant will chuckle. A modest superiority has thereby been charted, which it would be paradoxical to term control or mastery in an organism that is as yet incapable of exerting either; but it can safely be described as a narrow brush with loss of control audibly feted.

In relation to children, the matter stands otherwise; it can, at any rate, be stated positively. In "Ego Development and the Comic," Ernst Kris makes the valuable observation that children do not laugh at the so-called childish mispro-

[3] L. A. Sroufe, E. Water, and L. Matas, "Contextual Determinants of Infant Affective Response," in *The Origins of Fear* (New York: Wiley, 1974), cited in summary form in McGhee ("Children's Humour" 200).

nunciation of others until they themselves have mastered the difficulty. We may say, after the fact, that it stands to reason that they wouldn't, but the observation nevertheless establishes on a firm basis the equation of superiority with, in this case, hard-won assurance of safety with respect to a given infirmity. No case better approximates Hobbes's model: children, *cet âge est sans pitié* (that age knows no pity), are the Hobbesians par excellence. No case more plainly sets on view the connection of that superiority with the peace of mind required to allow one a good laugh at a disability not so long ago incurred. That the infirmity was once shared renders it more euphorically risible. Superiority here borders on an inferiority hastily plastered over. At all events, it goes into the making of that short-lived invulnerability in which laughter causes us to rejoice.

To be sure, the aggressive component of laughter must not be left out of reckoning. Plato's point, that we laugh at the weak without fear of retaliation, brings home the charge of hostility for which laughter secures impunity. Children promptly, loudly, and insistently deride the "childishness" of other children younger in age or accomplishment. Uninhibited by considerations of prudence or fellow feeling born of repeated experience of one's own risibility, they display mockery in its pure state of naked rejoicement in a failure not one's own. Their penchant for violence in the portrayal of mishaps—witness their delight in the mindless mayhem of the Three Stooges, their affection for Tom and Jerry cartoons, in which the cat invariably ends up plastered onto the ground—reinforces the sense that "primitively" (assuming the child in us to be the primitive par excellence) the comic was no more than wild aggression thinly veiled.

Aristotle must here be called to the rescue once more. The callousness may well be real, but the violence has been significantly altered. The Stooges may hit each other painful blows, but the cudgel rebounds off their wooden cranium, and the face of these literal blockheads registers nothing resembling human pain. Flattened one moment against the pavement, Jerry resumes his full-blown shape in the next frame, in time to mull over his next bit of nefariousness. Painlessness stands guard over the violence it renders permissible. To the degree that it *is* aggression, laughter remains a privileged aggression, watched over by a consciousness of inconsequentiality. That the consequences may seem real to others is largely beside the humorous point.

If we may speak of comic purgation, "What," asks Maurice Charney, "are we purged of? . . . the kinds of anxieties, aggressions, and repressions that constitute the demons of daily life" ("Comic Creativity" 2:39). Occasions for laughter are therefore sought out both to vent aggression and to still anxiety in a brief release from care, on wings of that imagined invulnerability that is the laughing mode. Kris, once more, states it compendiously when he notes that "the telling of a joke affects the listener like an invitation to common aggression and common regression" (Socarides 91). A childlike state is induced, of which I say more later in this chapter, which seals the compact of laughter in a healing irresponsibility, a pause that refreshes more surely than any carbonated beverage.

The spectator's detachment, which gives her leave to partake of the feast of laughter on stage, is yet another mode of comic purgation, according to Karlheinz Stierle: "The laughter of comedy is cathartic inasmuch as it allows the spectator to shed the human, all-too-human side of which he partakes himself, at the same time as the distance from the stage casts him into the fictional role of those Olympian gods to whom all was a joyous spectacle" (375). Pain disembodied by its remove from us, transmuted into a spectacle that invites detachment, is yet another modality of "superiority," the godlike serenity that lifts us above the fray, uninvited as we are to join in.

Perhaps the most direct evidence of the connection of laughter with aggressivity is supplied by observations in the realm of psychopathology. Michel Schwiech notes that in the treatment of psychopathic rage a corner is turned when a reason is discovered that allows the patient to laugh: "Laughter appears . . . at the moment that the subject in his aggressive encounter with the world, a maximum aggressivity, discovers and rediscovers an *intermediary* which allows him to render that aggressivity acceptable. . . . Laughter allows the patient to pass beyond an impossible aggressivity, a paralyzing anxiety, in an activity that is eminently pragmatic and joyful" (133). No greater violence can be imagined than that of a psychopath: the term was coined expressly to designate unhinged behavior. That laughter intervenes as a rational alternative, as a way to process excessive rage and channel it into harmless and constructive ends, meets head-on the paradox set up by the Hobbesian view. Far from being solely the expression of our aggressive nature, laughter is, in part, an outlet for, or if you will a transformer of, the aggressive impulse, dissipating it in euphoria. What pain laughter may inflict it is largely unaware of, except in the unrepresentative case of mockery and derision, where clear intent to wound runs counter to the spontaneity of unpremeditated mirth.

To sum up, then, Hobbes's "sudden glory," insofar as it can serve as a guide to the nature of laughter, highlights two related aspects of the phenomenon, which it tends to obscure by lumping together in an image of superiority. A momentary invulnerability that permits the laugher to shake in mirth unguardedly is one. A mitigated aggressivity, which translates physically into the loud assertiveness of the guffaw and which lends added zest to the laugh at an opponent's expense, is the other. The be-all of laughter is not to be found in that aggressiveness, but the idea of the victory of something over something else is inseparable from any occasion for hilarity.

*

The name of Alexander Bain, though less resonant than that of Hobbes, is quite as indissolubly attached to a view of the matter that could be fairly described as the flip side of the superiority theory. In *The Emotions and the Will* (1859), Bain asserted that "the occasion of the Ludicrous is the Degradation of some person or interest possessing dignity, in circumstances that excite no other emotion" (14.39). Aristotle may once again be invoked as having been the original promoter of that view, for he describes comedy as "representing men as worse" (*Poetics* 2.1) than they are in actual life. That laughter degrades, that it tears down what is generally deemed of value, or, in the view of the Stagirite, that humanity needs to be caricatured to be found laughable is the common tenor of the formulations that may be grouped under this head. The accent is on destructiveness, on a rebelliousness directed at what in the writer's estimation deserves respect. Hegel is particularly transparent in that regard: the common people, he notes with some distaste "often laugh at the most important and profound matters if they see in them only some wholly insignificant aspect which contradicts their habits and day-to-day outlook. In such a case laughter is only an expression of self-complacent wit, a sign that they are clever enough to recognize a contrast and are aware of the fact." He then goes on to outline a more acceptable mode of risibility, in an earlier version of the full-blown distinction devised by Etienne Souriau between brute and aesthetic laughter: "On the other hand, the comical as such implies an infinite light-heartedness and confidence felt by someone raised altogether above his own inner contradiction, and not bitter or miserable in it at all: this is the bliss and ease of a man who, being sure of himself, can bear the frustration of his aim and achievement" (2:1200). It sounds for all the world like the victory of the aggrieved metaphysician, who manages to laugh at his annoyance with those who cackle and jeer at his near impenetrable disclosure of the most important and profound matters. Be that as it may, the movement is instructive, from the disparagement of "ignorant" laughter to the recognition of a buoyancy in mirth that is not incompatible with the higher values that laughter, perceived as at someone's or something's expense, was felt to have manhandled.

Bergson's *mécanique plaqué sur du vivant* catches up in a vivid phrase the sense of fragility that presides over this approach to laughter and the comic, so akin to the revulsion chronicled by the Bossuets and Chesterfields of the preceding chapters. In a philosophy of vitalism such as Bergson promoted, what could be thought of as of higher worth than the adaptive suppleness of life itself? To see it encroached upon by the rigidly mechanical prompted the move to enlist laughter as a corrective. It is a corrective that, oddly enough, we seek out every occasion to apply: any lapse, any mildly reprehensible form of degradation, will do. Far from wishing to stamp them out, we take added delight in their every occurrence. It cannot have escaped even Bergson that we like to laugh and pay others to give us the chance to do so often.[4]

The most remarkable application of the degradation theory was made by Herbert Spencer, who based on it a comprehensive physiological model for the laughter mechanism that has proved enduring. It is the model that Freud, among others, adhered to in formulating his own views on the comic. In his essay "The Physiology of Laughter"

---

[4] See Berlyne (796), considered further in Chapter 6.

(1860), Spencer describes laughter as a discharge of accumulated nervous energy into channels leading to muscular agitation. He notes that it is an agitation bereft of purpose, and that it follows a path of least resistance, proceeding from the well-worn track that leads to the muscles involved in speech and the respiratory system to end up agitating the limbs and the trunk, arching the spine and bending back the head. An excess of energy thus overflows into those channels of habitual muscular action most readily open to it. The surplus energy thus suddenly rendered useless Spencer traces back to a sum of attention, of emotional concentration abruptly dissipated by a sudden drop in level, reducing expectation to little or nothing: as when a kid gambols on stage to lick the lovers' faces in a scene of romantic passion (his own example).

The crude energetics of such a model, grounded in the physics of the day, has made way for a more up-to-date formulation, as we find in the pages of Frederick R. Stearns, citing W. S. McCulloch: "The question of psychic energy . . . [is] better quantified . . . not in terms of energy, which is certainly wrong for the nervous system, but in terms of the amount of information that can be handled, and is being handled by those circuits which are free to work" (34).

Other models still current these days hinge on the quantification of arousal. Paul McGhee, reviewing experiments designed to measure degrees of arousal connected with the experience of funniness, notes a positive correlation among heart rate, galvanic skin response amplitude, muscle tension, and respiratory changes that appears to denote heightened arousal as an accompaniment of that experience. He goes on to speculate that the reason for the "mysterious" connection of humor with "the motor response of laughter . . . may lie in our general tendency to increase physical activity in states of heightened emotional arousal. In threatening situations this activity probably originally took the form of 'fight or flight.' The use of energy through physical exertion may aid in the process of returning arousal to a normal adaptive range, regardless of the particular form of that exertion ("Role of Arousal" 20). He then cites S. S. Tomkins to the effect that "laughter and other positive affects result from changes in neural firing that accompany *sudden drops in stimulation*" (21), a view that returns us to the general outlook of the degradation theory. Caution is sounded, however, when McGhee notes that, "while it is commonly acknowledged . . . that there are several forms of nonhumorous as well as humorous laughter, virtually no attempt has been made to study how these different kinds of laughter differ. It would be of immense value to the progress of humor research," he ruefully concludes, "if humorous could be distinguished either behaviorally or physiologically from other forms of laughter" (21). We see in the next chapter that a cognitive approach to the nature of laughter yields a similar tension/relaxation pattern, as the effort to resolve the puzzle of the joke yields to the pleasurable resolution of the punch line, experienced as a drop in intellectual tension.

A climax of sorts is reached in the representation of laughter as a process of degradation—or, more accurately, as the audible endorsement of an event so interpreted—in the theory propounded by Charles Lalo. While positing value as a given in all fields of human endeavor, Lalo assigns to aesthetic laughter the function of "permanent critique of all values" (22). In a "counterpoint" theory of art, wherein any object can be given value and every value can be turned into a nonvalue, "the equation of aesthetic laughter reads as 'Contrast + Degradation = Devaluation'" (33). The docker guffaws at the pommaded dude, the dude snickers at the other's grime, each in the name of a universal polyvalency of values that causes there to spring up "as many axes of up and down as there are value centers of gravitation" (90).

The shifting, unpredictable nature of laughter is thus given its due. The norms appealed to implicity by Aristotle, more explicitly by Bergson and Meredith, are not fixed once and for all, nor do they even operate unidirectionally. The sociology of laughter teaches us that laughter regulates the life of groups, ranging from the clique to the culture. As Montaigne put it, "there falls into man's imagination no fantasy so wild that it does not match the example of a public practice, and for which, consequently, our reason does not find a stay and a foundation" (*Complete Essays* 79). We are, in other words, a mutually risible lot.

Three variations on the motif of laughter incited by degradation offer us, respectively, a Christian, a folkloric, and a post-Nietzschean view of the matter. Ludovico Castelvetro, in his 1570 commentary on Aristotle's *Poetics,* advances the disabused observation that "our nature has been so corrupted by the sin of our first parents that we delight in seeing defects in our fellow men, either because the knowledge that others too are imperfect gives us the assurance that we are not as imperfect as we thought or because the perception in others of defects we do not possess ourselves makes us feel superior and fills us with pride and joy" (Lauter 95). Laughter either repairs or fortifies our self-esteem, so justly unhinged by the Fall: a view penitentially Hobbesian. Another's loss is thus our gain, in that middling zone where nothing too drastic is at stake.

The folk figure of fun of the cuckold, accentuated in French by the rising inflection on the acute vowel of the second syllable of the noun *cocu,* comes in for a lot of unfeeling fun, in Latin countries, practically to this day. Philip Stewart offers this explanation: "Cuckoldry is only funny because it has been made aseptic by other considerations: bourgeois status, jealousy, foolishness, etc. It is related to forces of violence in human society, but it lacks violence, in fact, and is only ridiculous because it is banal and powerless. The cuckold is unable to avenge himself, hence his fundamental clownishness" (202). We are reminded of Plato's implicit caveat: laugh only at those who can be depended on not to crack your pate. Laughter brings down what is impotent to begin with; the man who cannot hold his own wife is fair game, being inherently silly (a synonym, originally for weak), the more so when you consider that, in law at any rate, he holds all the trumps.

The nihilist streak in the present-day intellectual climate quite naturally lends a greater sweep to the supposed causticity of laughter: "What is comic, and what induces laughter, is that which brings out the void in what, officially, is valued, and the valuable in what, officially, ranks as void" (Marquard 141). In a culture of rebellion, laughter finds itself invested with a mission that goes well beyond its charter: that of a transvaluation of values, bringing down what is now high, setting up what was deemed low. The Lord of Misrule, however, is king only for a day. Laughter does briefly institute a world that is topsy-turvy; it does not erect inverted towers. Revolutionary fervor is as fair a target as establishment piety. *All* axes, as Lalo so aptly brings out, are at all times reversible. Laughter rejoices in that very instability.

*

The example Alexander Bain offers of his degradation theory is the spectacle of school children released from the oppressiveness of the classroom into the freedom of the playground, to the accompaniment of shrieks of laughter. The hint is reinforced in a study of preschoolers in which "the free play environment was found to have significantly lower rates of glee than the lesson environment" (Sherman 360). *Pr*eschoolers need not await the bell to initiate decompressive moves. As a paradigm of enforced behavior, the schoolroom thus invites a shift from the aggrieved view of laughter as tearing down something "possessing dignity" to its function as decompressant,[5] a shift, in other words, from degradation theory to libertarian outlook. The tinge of disapproval implicit in the very titles affixed to earlier views—superiority, degradation—gives way to positive endorsement of laughter in the view that identifies it in various ways with human freedom. The spontaneity, the unforced character of what on that account we call genuine laughter, its apparent gratuitousness,[6] gives it the character of "a continuing bodily metaphor for freedom" (Pollio 215). Its euphoric tonality, moreover, offers it as the ringing assertion of the self's integrity in the face of grim necessity, momentarily held at bay. The freedom of laughter, it must be added, finds its dovetailing confirmation in the laughing character ascribed to freedom itself, in this remarkable passage from George Santayana: "Free life has the spirit of comedy. It rejoices in the seasonable beauty of each new thing, and laughs at its decay, covets no possessions, demands no agreement, and strives to sustain nothing except a gallant spirit of courage and truth, as each fresh adventure may renew it" (102–3). The smile of Socrates clearly shows through this moving philosophical credo, which lodges the spirit of laughter at the heart of our understanding of spirit itself, in the guise of spiritedness.

Undoubtedly the most celebrated name that attaches to a consideration of laughter as a modality of freedom is that of Sigmund Freud. An early work, whose title I give in the original for reasons that soon become apparent, *Der Witz und seine Beziehung zum Unbewussten* (1903), and the later

---

[5] "Laughter is an expansive movement, it is also a *decompressant*. It is not only an expansion, it is also a relief" (Lorge 76).

[6] "On the functional plane, laughter is a purely gratuitous act" (Monnier 61).

essay "Humor" (1928) represent his contribution to the understanding of laughter. *Der Witz* has been variously translated as "wit" (A. A. Brill) or "jokes" (James Strachey). Neither term quite hits the mark, in a striking illustration of the problem of nomenclature adverted to by Olivier Revault d'Allonnes (see Chapter 1). "Jest" is probably close, but it carries a faintly archaic air; the French "bon mot" may be the nearest we can come to conveying the idea of a joke that mostly hinges on a happy turn of phrase.

Taking as a starting point Spencer's account of the physiology of laughter, which rests upon a descending contrast in the risible event, Freud goes on to posit an economy in psychic expenditure which liberates the sum of nervous energy that pours itself out in laughter. Wit and dreams, he points out, make use of identical techniques such as condensation, displacement, nonsense, and indirect expression. Forbidden impulses (obscene, aggressive) are thus ferried past the Censor in tendentious wit as they are in dreams, dissipating attention by the gift of forepleasure delivered by the cleverness of these maneuvers. A deeper pleasure thereupon results from lifted inhibitions, in both the wit and her audience. In the case of an innocent jest, of a *mot d'enfant*, pleasure in nonsense results from tapping the roots of a primitive freedom, that of the child as yet unburdened by the rule of reason, able therefore to play with sounds regardless of meaning. All we know of the world, a word's "pragmatic associations," may thus be freely set aside in loose association and oneiric fantasy. As to the comic, which Freud rather awkwardly dissociates from both wit and humor, confining it to slapstick and pratfall,[7] he sees in it the economy of the psychic expenditure invested in representation, an economy that springs

---

[7] See Jean Guillaumin's able critique of that oddity in "Freud entre les deux topiques."

from the comparison of the adult I am with the child stomping on the stage. The clown exerts himself mightily, like a child unaware of the true dimensions of the object he wrestles with. As a grown-up, I am spared the sympathetic representation of that useless effort. There occurs therefore a "degradation to being a child," of which Freud cannot decide whether it "is only a special case of comic degradation, or whether everything comic is based fundamentally on degradation to being a child" (*Jokes* 227–28). But in a celebrated concluding paragraph, the father of analysis returns wit, comic, and humor to that primal condition unambiguously:

> The pleasure in jokes has seemed to us to arise from an economy in expenditure upon inhibition, the pleasure in the comic from an economy in expenditure upon ideation (upon cathexis) and the pleasure in humour from an economy upon feeling. All three are agreed in representing methods of regaining from mental activity a pleasure which has in fact been lost through the development of that activity. For the euphoria which we endeavor to reach by these means is nothing other than the mood of a period of life in which we were accustomed to deal with our psychical work in general with a small expenditure of energy—the mood of our childhood, when we were ignorant of the comic, when we were incapable of jokes and when we had no need of humour to make us feel happy in our life. (236)

Behind, and beyond, the evident nostalgia of this striking declaration may be glimpsed a vision of the higher functions of our intellectual apparatus (to borrow his metaphor) somewhat in the position of an advanced, complex civilization yearning for the simplicities of its rural past, a Rousseauesque vision of lost authenticity and lost freedom. Interestingly enough, the sense of a split—of an opposition within our psychic life between the spontaneity of childhood, surviving in attenuated form, and the complex apparatus of the higher functions—is a sense to be met with as well in the contemporaneous findings of American psychology, then in its infancy. Stanley Hall and Arthur Allin, in "The Psychology of Tickling and Laughter," conclude that "these minimal touch excitations . . . represent the very oldest stratum of psychic life in the soul, and have still in their strange sensitiveness and energy reminiscences of the primeval vigor and spontaneity of the dawn of psychic life . . . in the world" (12). From ontogeny to phylogeny, from childhood to the so-called childhood of the race, the two accounts echo one another: laughter taps a vigor and a spontaneity which intellect and civilization imperfectly subdue—it is, in fact, amid the constraints and repressions of civilized existence, the buoyant expression of an earlier freedom.

What D. H. Monro characterizes as the "tangled skein" (190–91) of Freud's understanding of psychic economy has also been criticized by Tzvetan Todorov as faulty rhetorical analysis.[8] George McFadden brushes it aside altogether: "The whole conception of cathectic expenditure and saving . . . is really only a metaphor. . . . Judged . . . aesthetically, the metaphor is old-fashioned and unattractive, indeed rather self-contradictory, since it is the prodigal expense rather than the saving that relates most truly to our sense of the comic" (137). Laughter for him, then, is "a movement of prodigality and spendthrift abandonment." Though Freud might object that what is being dispensed so freely was made available for dissipation by a previous accumulation, made possible by a previous saving, it is clear that the main point in either view is the gratuitous expenditure, whatever its derivation.

---

[8] Todorov, "Recherches sur le symbolisme linguistique: Le mot d'esprit et ses rapports avec le symbolique," *Poétique* 8 (1974): 215–45.

Two complementary modes of the position that laughter can be envisaged as liberation may be illustrated, one by a restatement of its relation to the *Tendenz* (whether hostile or obscene) directly at odds with that of Freud, and the other from a neo-Aristotelian analysis of comedy.

Marie Ramondt writes, "What characterizes the comic impression is that we are plunged in the low, the vile, the repulsive, but that we do not remain stuck there. No sooner do we fall in, in fact, than we are fished out. It is that liberation that gives birth to laughter" (76). Does humor free us to be aggressive and obscene, or does it offer us the blessed relief of no more than passing contact with these dark energies, as we "get them out of our system"? The question is answerable only by an appeal to a hypothesized "human nature," which is given either to treasuring its hostilities or to renouncing them gladly. Creatures of contradiction that we are, we can safely be said to incline both ways at once, so there is scarcely a need to take sides. Laughter, on either view, is perceived as ex-pressive— freeing the organism of an inner pressure.

Outward pressure appears to be principally addressed in Elder Olson's remark that "the comic function is less one of producing laughter than one of producing a lightheartedness with which laughter is associated" (40). The remark has the virtue of addressing a perplexity of comedic (as against comic) theory: the undesirability of tying the success of comedy quantitatively to the production of laughter, in television sitcom fashion, the equal undesirability of severing comedy from the comic (turning it into a soap opera). Lightheartedness translates exactly to euphoria, the buoyancy of which laughter is the end product. The *weight* of care, the *pressure* of responsibility, are both images drawn from the physical law of gravity that holds us earthbound. The effervescence of gaiety and high spirits betokens, contrariwise, the kind of escape imaged for us by an upward flight of bubbles.

Freedom is heady stuff. Whether laughter returns us to the lightheartedness of childhood (ever ready to follow up tears with giggles), or whether it rings a brief respite from the iron law of necessity (Freud's celebrated reality principle), or whether it exorcises our forbidden thoughts for a brief spell by giving them licit passage into the open, the association of these various orders of release with an outburst itself both gratuitous and spontaneous marks out laughter as our invaluable talisman. It is the secret of enduring sanity in a world hedged with the threat of every horror, every ignominy, every agony in its capacious arsenal. Euphoria, as the heightened sense of our well-being, so clearly radiates from a laughing countenance that we have no trouble viewing it as the brief holiday from care that opens a window upon a better, freer existence.

So, at any rate, runs the positive reading of laughter, which we must be at pains to hold in conjunction with the earlier readings—superiority, degradation—which it modifies but does not altogether displace.

*

Freud's view that laughter returns us in a flash to the freedom of the little child unburdened by knowledge or experience, unshackled as yet by the inhibitions that weigh on civilized deportment, leads quite naturally to the possibility that it is a manifestation of the spirit of play. In his *Essay on Laughter* (1902), James Sully gave the connection its fullest elaboration, concluding that "the effect of the laughable . . . is a highly complex feeling, containing something of the child's joyous surprise at the new and unheard of; something too of the child's gay responsiveness to a play-challenge; often something also of the glorious sense of expansion after compression which gives the large mobility to freshly freed limbs of young animals and children"(153). Playfulness is certainly a disposition that leads to hilarity, and the decompressant function so much in evidence in the passage from the schoolroom to the playground is scarcely absent from the above-described medley. A more rigorous analysis of the moment of laughter, in Claude Saulnier's *Le sens du comique*, focuses on playful awareness:

> If he truly experiences the oscillation from the real to the unreal, if the fantasy unreal made him "stumble" [*trébucher*], if during the time of his surprise and the redress that followed that redress did not occur in logical fashion but in emotional fashion, causing the sense of the real and the sense of the fictitious to mingle in his soul as in the soul of a child, but with a keen awareness of that confusion, the auditor then laughs. He enjoys his own error and the redress that follows, experiencing the playful character of this dramatic oscillation, which then prolongs the joyous gasps of laughter. As it fastens on this very oscillation and on the pleasure of intellectual emotion, attention causes it to rebound. Hence those spasms that fall to rise again several times before dying out altogether. (31)

Made aware that it was for a moment taken in, consciousness seizes on the playful character of contradictory signals that come at it thus simultaneously. The resultant laughter reproduces in its spasmodic exhalations the mental back-and-forth of a painless error inflicted *pour rire*, for the fun of it.

For Elie Aubouin, the playful character of laughter is the positive counterpart of Aristotle's proviso that the comic be painless. The world *for fun* takes the place of the world *for real*, removes the sting of mortality, reenacts the fantasy world of make-believe. Reality is suspended for a spell, and the blows that rain on pates hurt no one. According to Max Eastman, on the other hand, it is *because* they are blows, though calculated to inflict no pain, that we laugh—in virtue of the principle that "it is the unpleasant in general which, when taken playfully, is enjoyed as funny" (8). Superiority and degradation thus once more take up their places in the constellation of the comic, this time in the company of play.

A certain playfulness can be detected in Freud's 1928 essay on humor, a term taken by him in the German sense of laughter in the teeth of disaster: rueful, one might say, or even gallows humor. In the book on wit an earlier triad had played out the following minidrama: a preconscious thought, dipping into the unconscious, reemerged into consciousness. That drama we find reassigned to a new cast of characters: "The humorous attitude . . . consists in the humorist's having withdrawn the physical accent from his ego and having transposed it to his super-ego. To the super-ego, thus inflated, the ego can appear tiny and all its interests trivial; and, with the new distribution of energy, it may become an easy matter for the super-ego to suppress the ego's possibilities of reacting" (21:164). The towering superego rests a hand on the tiny ego's shoulder, reasons with it gently: "Look! here is the world, which seems so dangerous. It is nothing but a game for children—just worth making a jest about" (21:166). A playful glance at the puny stage of our endeavors brings them "into perspective," the perspective of a perpetual children's hour where nothing can come about that need be taken to heart. Regression, invulnerability, superiority—all the old properties are wrapped up in a playfulness that lifts the weight of the world off our shoulders and gives us the last word when it rages at us ineffectually. The felon about to be hanged on a Monday who observes that the week begins badly trivializes his impending doom with a composure that gives him the laugh on it—and on us as well, if we have not the heart to chuckle.

A final observation concerning laughter in its relationship to play may fittingly be derived from Guillaumin's earlier-cited critique of Freud's treatment of the comic:

In a general way, and even when, as may happen, the "subject" and the "object" of the comic turn out to be one and the same person, *the comic presupposes a psychic distance between an observed and an observer.* It presupposes, on the other hand, and even when these characters are quite distinct one from the other, *a certain psychic participation of the observer with the observed.* (633)

The play of distance *and* participation, the fact that as we laugh we simultaneously enter into and reject the state of mind that was induced by, or that made possible, the misstep, the error, the blunder, does offer a rough parallel to the utter absorption and fundamental irrelevance that characterize our participation in a game. Whether the ball is caught or not, nothing "real" hangs on it—though a vast sum of money may change hands in an equally "unreal" gambling operation (a game by another name). Yet the contest is entered into in a spirit of life-and-death earnestness. Play, in other words, takes make-believe seriously, for the time being. Humor, on the other hand, takes reality playfully, making it do handsprings in the cause of mirthful laughter. A parallel is to be found between the two activities in a shared tolerance for unhurtful contradictoriness. Both partake, moreover, of a zestful spirit we associate with childhood, that heyday of zaniness when we were ever ready to laugh *and* play.[9]

How far have we traveled, in this chapter, in our quest for a rounded assessment of the phenomenon of laughter in relation to the comic?

[9] It strikes me, on rereading these lines on games, that, however spirited, they must be clearly distinguished from the often grim business of sporting contests—replete with mayhem and even death. Contests of skill originated in mock combat; many factors, prime among them the not always vicarious pugnacity of spectators, conspire to bring them uncomfortably close to the real thing. A game of tennis is not quite the same thing as a match played out before a huge and too often highly partisan crowd at Wimbledon or Seoul.

Strong convergences have made themselves manifest, balanced by equally powerful divergences. Superiority and degradation theories share a common terrain, that of laughter's anarchic potential, which tears down the one to set up the other. While Hobbes rejoices in the enhanced sense of self that laughs at the faults and blemishes of others, Hegel deplores the wanton desecration of that which is laughed at unjustly, mocked for being too good for this world. In either view laughter sounds the trumpet call of aggression. It both asserts and breaks down. The school of Spencer and Freud, on the other hand, lays stress on the relief if offers from the tyranny of the ought and the should, the pressures and responsibilities of adult life, the weight of inhibitions that hold down a natural exuberance. The exultation of laughter is not so much at another's cost, in this view, as it is a decided boon to all. It is the salute of an organism freed momentarily of its largely self-forged manacles. As such it is notoriously infectious. The euphoria this school of thought bespeaks as of the essence of the phenomenon spills over into a generalized spirit of play, whose exact line of demarcation is hard to draw. Laughter and play return us conjointly to the high spirits of childhood days, where even genuine hardship soon yields to the pervasive buoyancy of an untried organism, eager to run and shout and leap and bound all the livelong day. Energy expended for the joy of it in a kind of heedless triumph, sparked by the oddity of an unexpected (and somewhat justified) reversal (here I anticipate) may serve as a provisional statement of that particular segment of our progress.

CHAPTER FOUR

Laughter Sparked:
A Binary-Structural Approach

Deux visages semblables dont aucun ne fait rire en particulier, font rire ensemble par leur ressemblance. [Two faces are alike; neither is funny by itself, but side by side their likeness makes us laugh.]

—Blaise Pascal

That is what a joke is—getting somebody going and then leaving him up in the air.

—Max Eastman

The explanatory mode most in tune with contemporary habits of thought presides over a cluster of theories that set aside putative function or emotive coloration to fasten on the intellectual character of what Saulnier termed an intellectual emotion. Laughter, in this view, is occasioned by the perception of a contrast. The *intellectualist* theories seek a rigorous description of that contrast, looking as they do to the binary structure of the event that triggers laughter for an understanding of the phenomenon. Immanuel Kant's name flies on the banner that flutters over these views, the Königsberg sage having in the *Critique of Judgment* defined the comic as "an intense expectation that comes to nothing."[1] Pascal, before him, had already af-

---

[1] "Das Lachen ist ein Affekt aus der plötzlichen Verwandlung einer gespannten Erwartung in nichts" (Kant, *Kritik der Urtheilskraft* 333).

84

firmed in the eleventh Provincial Letter that "it is impossible that . . . such a surprise not cause laughter inasmuch as
nothing so much moves that way as a surprising disproportion between what we expect and what we see" (*Les
provinciales* 5:316). The surprise of an unlooked-for drop in
the level of attention required, in relation to the sum of
attention mobilized, leaves us prey to helpless laughter if it
is sudden enough.

Pascal speaks of disproportion. Kant implies disappointment: we were all set to apprehend "something" and find
ourselves holding "nothing." The mind is fooled, the wind
taken out of us, painlessly—for the "disappointment" is far
from grievous. The contrast, at all events, is a descending
one: *some*thing makes way for *no*thing. Incongruity implies
a derogation from the congruous, from that which holds
together in the mind as fitting. Pascal's opponents had
prepared the world for a momentous issue of faith and
fobbed it off with an idle play on words—the descent is
abrupt.

A more neutral, less openly downward-directional formulation appears to remove the risible from the realm of
judgment to that of simple value-free contradiction. We
laugh, writes Léon Dumont, "when our understanding is
set up to take in two contradictory relationships simultaneously" (20). We find this view beautifully laid out and
analyzed in the following passage by Ramon Fernandez:

> To take something seriously is to be conscious of its reality. To
> be conscious of an event that "takes place" before us is to
> believe that it could not be felt, or seen, or conceived differ-
> ently *at the moment and from the point of view* that we occupy.
> The consciousness of the reality of a thing leads us, spectator
> though we be, to a kind of active participation. . . . The func-
> tion of laughter is clear: it consists in breaking up this at-one-
> ness with things, this communion with the real.

That is the result of laughter, but how is it obtained? By a hundred different devices each of which gave us a theory. But all these devices resemble each other in the effect they bring about: they suddenly introduce into ourselves a view of the event that is different, and even the opposite, from the view the event had suggested. We are so constituted, however, that we cannot hold two opposed views of the same thing at the same moment: hence that sensation of a slide, of a drop, of a dissolution that accompanies laughter. (75)

Charles Lalo calls "irrealists" those who, like Fernandez and Saulnier, view the contrast as bringing into question for the laugher the reality of the real itself. In this line of thinking Marc Chapiro goes to the limit: the comic, as he sees it, introduces into the consciousness of the laugher the perception of the absurd by way of paralogical moves that elude the logical censor. The end result is the irradiation of the real by the absurd in a consciousness that consigns the whole universe to that condition. Hence the sense of relaxation, the relief experienced by the laugher, liberated by the comic from her existential angst, the "fear of life" that the real inspires (52–56).

There is little left here of the ostensible repudiation of directionality in the contrast. The contrast of real and unreal can scarcely be put down as the purely lateral collision of equal partners. Neither the escape from the real, nor the successful challenge to an "at-one-ness" enforced by the perception that the world is out there for us to deal with, can be viewed as value neutral. By some kind of illusionism we are allowed to slip for a spell the weight of things-as-they-are off our shoulders. A nothing has clearly displaced a something, that something being no less than the sum of all things.

Such generalizing, or in Chapiro's case we might say totalizing, vagaries contrast with the more clean-cut specifications embraced by, say, Bergson. It will be remembered that laughter was moved, in this view, by the sight of a live body bouncing like an object, with the rigidity, the abruptness, of *du mécanique plaqué sur du vivant*. The jack-in-the-box gave a good sense of the kind of springlike, repetitive, unadapted motion that mocked the fluid suppleness of the live human body it caricatured. A Molière character hung up on his idée fixe or a circus clown tripping over herself or collapsing like a sack of potatoes could similarly "crack us up" by turning a live person into some sort of a thing. A slip up, a stumble, a faux pas, all lapses from the adaptive, all fell under the correction of salutary hilarity.

The schematic character of such a pattern points to a weakness in this type of explanation: its tendency to over-intellectualize the issue. Deprived of its emotional coloration, shorn of mirth, laughter, reduced to a judgment, charged with disapproval, does not much resemble what we experience under that name. The two terms contrasted, moreover, inhabit too predictable a space in the writer's own pantheon of values: the high of adaptive vitality tripped up by the low of mechanical rigidity. Others will read the matter otherwise, but their binary schema will identically reflect the pattern of their own intellectual preferences. We have seen the Victorian Bain contrasting an object "possessing dignity" with the urchin's unholy glee, Hegel ruefully assigning laughter to the scoffs of the small-minded in the face of the Ideal. For Schopenhauer the concrete fact (slipping on a banana peel) runs counter the general expectation (that men walking on a city street will remain upright): the mind is tripped up and we laugh. Intellect is no match for brute occurrence. A rationalist such as Marie Swabey, on the other hand, draws a rationalist moral from the affair: "It is far from being the case that the transformation of an anticipatory judgment into nothing gives pleasure because of a wholesome shock to the body. The fact is that the discovery of mistakes is painful, although the *correction* of an error by the understanding gives satisfaction as making for the victory of reason over unreason in the world (107). The polarity of the worse and the grander, the former getting the better of the latter, is a pretty standard one in comic theory, however, as we see in Chapter 6.

A couple of apparent exceptions to what we may want to call a value-laden polarity formulation deserve a closer look. Arthur Koestler, in *The Act of Creation*, rewrites an earlier distinction of his in the following terms: "The sudden bisociation of an event with two habitually incompatible matrices will produce a comic effect, provided that the narrative . . . carries the right kind of emotional tension" (51). The proviso is a large and indefinite one: it quietly begs the question of the ostensibly neutral scientific phraseology, the learned talk of bisociations and matrices. Looked at more closely, the description is revealed to assume a directional arrow. "The right kind of emotional tension," in an earlier, more explicit formulation, takes on a decidedly Hobbesian character: "The necessary and sufficient conditions which define the nature of the comic stimulus are the sudden bisociation of a junctional idea or event with two independent operative fields, *and the presence of a dominant aggressive component in the compound emotional charge*" (*Insight and Outlook* 1:171, emphasis added).

Closely related, G. B. Milner's statement, "Within a single situation and a single linguistic context, two universes collide, and it is this collision that makes many forms of humour possible" (16), is liable to the same stricture. "Many forms" is prudently indefinite, and some "universes" of discourse may be imagined to collide unfunnily (the lover's fiery passion, the confessor's hellfire, *if taken to heart*). Emotional underpinnings must be assumed, and sorted out.

No more value-neutral language exists than the mathematical. I owe to John W. Paulos the suggestion that a topological theory developed by the French mathematician René Thom in 1975, catastrophe theory, which deals with the "description and classification of such discontinuities (jumps, switches, reversals) provides a sort of mathematical metaphor for the structure of humor" (75). A detailed account of Thom's theorem is beyond the requirements of this survey: the reader is referred to Paulos's lucid and compendious presentation (75–99). Suffice it to say that the way an ambiguity leads to a sudden jump, a switch of meanings, as in a pun or a joke, is represented by the model as a cusp-shaped curve. A critical increase in one of the two values involved in the ambiguity precipitates a drop from upper to lower layer in the cusp. As Paulos describes it, "A joke . . . depends on the perception of incongruity in a given situation or its description. A joke can thus be considered a kind of structured ambiguity, the punch line precipitating the catastrophe of switching interpretations. It adds sufficient information to make it suddenly clear that the second (usually hidden) meaning is the intended one" (85). *Catastrophe* is Greek for downturn or downfall. A pun, such as the one Paulos cites in illustration, W. C. Fields's bludgeon of a reply to an innocuous query ("Do you consider clubs appropriate for small children?—Only when kindness fails"), leaves us in no doubt of the *direction* of the switch. In Paulos's own phrase, "a catastrophic fall from the upper to the lower layer of the graph." Even graphs, therefore, know of an upper and a lower: the comic remains safely in the realm of value, associated not with a rise but with a drop.

That the drop be sudden is a prescription routinely adhered to by theoreticians of every persuasion (see, in particular, Hobbes and Koestler). A word is in order about that requirement. Dupréel adduces a quaint example to illustrate what he calls the *rire d'accueil*, the laughter that knits a collection of individuals into a group. Someone sits down in a streetcar at a seat above which the roof leaks. His fellow passengers watch the drop form over his head in gleeful anticipation. The drop falls at last on his neck, to the release of pent-up breath in a general outburst of laughter. Conversation ensues among these strangers on the deplorable state of the rolling stock and so on. The scene, it must be remembered, is set in France, where easy intercourse among strangers is a rarity and where it would perhaps occur to no one to warn the fellow to move. What is at issue in this example, however, is the status of the surprise element in the definition of the laugh-provoking, of the comic. Clearly the fall of the drop is fully anticipated by all who will laugh at it. The surprise is for the victim (as in all practical jokes, so-called) and is precisely what is laughed *at*. In an ordinary, garden variety sort of joke the punch line delivers its punch to the listener; she laughs at having been thus harmlessly taken in and then taken aback. The teller joins in from contagion and from being caught up in the drama of her own making. Yet we are also all familiar with the careful buildup, in farce say, where a character is visibly being set up for a kick in the pants that is the more delectable to see administered as we have been made to await it with almost painful certainty. The point of this antithetical procedure lies, does it not, in the one uncertainty that does make the awaited climax come as a surprise: the exact moment of its long-anticipated fall. We watch the drop form but when it finally hits we ourselves are taken aback that it fell when at last it did. We had almost given up hope.

Whether the surprise takes the form of the unexpected reemergence, in the punch line of a joke, of an artfully concealed line of thought that the context had imparted without seeming to do so—the word *club*, with its potential for switching from association to cudgel—or whether we receive the shock of passing abruptly from the anticipation that something may happen at any moment to the realization that it *has* happened at *this* moment, the clash of near-opposites that we call incongruity catches our ear or our eye in an instant. It is, you could say, in the nature of an explosion to be set off by a spark.

Surprise, I might add, supplies the place of emotion in the binary scheme of the structural-intellectualist approach. The joyous sense of having been had—in no very material sense, however—and having gotten over it allows even the victim to join in with the spectators of a mild discomfiture that took them also by surprise; join them, that is, in a good laugh at his own expense. The cost in frayed dignity is more than made up for by the mildness of the offense, the pleasure in rising superior to it, the boon of companionship in laughter. The shock has turned into a tickle.

Jean Fourastié affirms that laughter arises out of a break in determinism (*une rupture de déterminisme,* 25). An important modification must be entered on such a simplified summary of the matter. We find it aptly and economically put in an essay by Siegfried J. Schmidt with the imposing title "Komik als Beschreibungsmodell kommunikativer Handlungsspiele" (The Comic as Descriptive Model of Communication Games). Schmidt speaks of the punch line flaring out of the hitherto obscured second line of the narrative (the second term of Paulos's "ambiguity") as *das Unerwartete aber doch Bekannte und daher Erkennbare*–the unexpected that is nonetheless known and hence recognizable (188). The comic surprise administers a shock of recognition. We always knew that *club* also meant *cudgel:* how silly of us to let our attention wander, not to have been more on our guard when in the presence of none other than W. C. Fields. The telling of a joke is by its very nature a challenge, an announcement that something is sneaking up on us and will pop out, taking us—though fairly and

more than fairly put on notice—unawares. Too much alert-
ness would only spoil the fun, so we enter into our role as
dupe with all the good will that goes into every other sort
of make-believe, playing blithely into the hand of the James
Sully school of laughter as play.

It is not enough, therefore, for the joke, the pun, the slip
up, as some would have it, to frustrate expectation and
rupture the determinism: it must be richly done. Our sense
of the fitness of things must be appealed to, at least when
we are not in the mood to laugh at just anything said to
provoke a laugh. There is, in the normal course, a resistance to be overcome by he who would throw us off our
tracks: we must land where we are pleased to find ourselves—fittingly, that is.[2] Yes, clubs exist to beat us as well
as to be joined by us, and W. C. Fields is the man for
whom that meaning would be paramount. There is recognition both of the forgotten resourcefulness of the language,
packing two disparate meanings into one word, *and* of the
mock-ferocity of the persona, of which we also took insuffi-
cient notice. Their coming together packs matter enough for
an explosion: a chuckle at least, if not a guffaw.

A kind of logic must prevail over the illogic of the juxtaposition: our reason, if it is to be taken in, must be given at
least mock-reasonable grounds. A sop, we might well call
it, to the rationalists.

An apparent counterexample provides us with both an
elegant confirmation of the descriptive validity of incongruity theory and a subtler restatement of the foregoing
"method-in-madness" rumination. As reported by J. H.
Goldstein, the Swedish experimentalist G. Nerhardt
"adapted a familiar psychophysical task to the study of

[2] D. H. Monro puts it quite precisely: "The laughable is a species of the
inappropriate. If we go on to ask the differentia, it resides . . . in this, that
there is an element of appropriateness in the inappropriate, when it is
funny" (255).

laughter by varying the last weight in a graded series of lifted weights and recording the amount of smiling and laughter elicited by weights of varying discrepancy from the series. He reports that laughter increased as the last weight varied from the subjects' expectations" (170). One imagines the burly young gymnast, poised for what promises to be the really taxing effort crowning a series of graduated grunts, finding himself practically lifted off the ground by the unopposed upward swing of bulging arm and shoulder muscles. What an exhilarating comedown!

The point of the experiment no doubt resides in the quantification of incongruity or, if you will, frustrated expectation. The greater the discrepancy, the bigger the laugh. Its homelier virtue is the compelling physical model it offers of the risible properties of an abruptly descending contrast. No more "objective" representation of that principle at work could easily be imagined.

Yet where do we locate the hidden familiarity to which the unexpected reversal (from ever steeper effort, to no effort at all) is supposed to return us? in what way is the drop in weight a return to a condition of which we should not have so entirely lost sight? where, in other words, is the other term of the ambiguity, originally ignored, explosively reasserting itself in the resolution?

The baffled athlete, if he is not to get angry at having been trifled with, has but one place to go to locate and evaluate the blame for his vanished challenge: humorous intent. He took for granted that the experiment he had been engaged for was a serious one. He had not reckoned with the possibility that it was a serious investigation of the unserious—or even of the larger, metaphysical possibility that things at no point are guaranteed to be what they seem. . . . That ever-present second line in the ontological narrative he had unwittingly allowed to catch up with him.

Two extended citations from the writings of Paul Mc-

Ghee, the first one to be relished as much for the quaint-
ness of its language as for the valuable point it makes, can
help us look at the binary schema of incongruity from the
aspect of the mental-emotional prerequisites of its effective-
ness.

First, from "On the Cognitive Origins of Incongruity
Humor: Fantasy Assimilation versus Reality Assimilation":

> It is hypothesized here that conceptual thinking is a neces-
> sary cognitive prerequisite for the experience of humor based
> on violation of cognitive expectancies. The possession of con-
> cepts is essential to the development in a child of a sense of
> confidence or certainty regarding his growing knowledge of his
> environment; and a high level of cognitive mastery over differ-
> ent aspects of the environment is postulated here as being a
> necessary, but not sufficient, prerequisite for the identification
> of humor in the representation of the environment in a manner
> which is inconsistent with the child's prior experience and
> acquired concepts regarding it. In short, in order for the
> violation of cognitive expectancies to be perceived as funny,
> the child must be sufficiently certain of the way the depicted
> elements actually occur to assure himself that the events
> simply do not occur as depicted. (66)

To the reader's belated relief, the last sentence manages to
boil down into almost straightforward English the laborious
development of the preceding paragraph. It all comes per-
ilously close to a truism: it is hard to violate expectancies
that just aren't there.

The point, for all that, is not so trivial as this may make
it sound. Humor is an acquired taste, acquired on the basis
of a requisite mental sophistication. Incongruities do not
occur in nature, as Bergson noted, they occur in the mind.
Our conceptual grids for the ordering and retrieval of experience must be momentarily interfered with, or rather

caused to work against themselves, for a halt to be called, a reordering to be invited, that briefly foregrounds the process itself and its inherent limitations. Small children go into gales of laughter by simply violating a taboo—in our own childish vocabulary, a no-no—pulling down their pants or emphatically calling attention by name to one or the other excretory function: they make do with what clash of ought and deed comes to hand. Clearly it takes greater conceptual savoir faire to rise to less homely juxtaposition. "Why does the fireman wear red suspenders?" sends the mind on a track of a potential symbolism: the color red figures in the fireman's equipment, is not unrelated to his metier; it is a notorious attention getter (red flag, red light). —"To hold up his pants" operates a switch from the symbolic to the homely which rests on an obviously enlarged mental catalog, taking in the slipperiness of that fulcrum of explanatory exploration, why?, as well as the two worlds of uniformed public service and vestimentary decorum.

The second citation from McGhee, on the other hand, enlarges our purview from intellect to imagination:

> In . . . fantasy activities . . . a new set of 'rules' seems available to the child, such that discrepant ideas or events may be assimilated into a given concept of schema without attempting to accommodate the schema to fit the peculiar properties of the new event. . . . It is this capacity for pretending that an object or event has certain characteristics, with full awareness that it does not, which enables the child to perceive certain such juxtapositions as being humorous. ("Origins and Early Development of Incongruity-Based Humour" 30)

In addition to bringing out the relationship of the comic to the imagination, to the ability, that is, to hold to two views of the same event, one of them made up, without confusing them,[3] this passage presents a model of the relationship postulated earlier of laughter to play. From make-believe, humor grows. The mind-set that invents impossible juxtaposition (this cardboard box is my castle) is all set to rejoice at an unanticipated conflation that on some fragile ground of logic manages for an instant to seem to hold water, taking the mind in by an artful though improbable fiction.

Laughter's connection with that momentary leap from one level to another in a binary formation receives its consecration at the earliest point in the human ontogeny from a study of earliest smiles and earliest laughter by Anthony Ambrose. Under "stimulation . . . at intermediate intensity . . . the smiling movements that develop long before smiling becomes a response specifically to the human face in the fifth week . . . are precursors not only of the smiling response but also of the later developing laughing response: they are in fact low intensity laughing" (178). But this "low intensity" response does not turn into full-bodied laughter "until about the fourth month of life precisely because the infant's capacity for ambivalence only becomes fully developed at that age-level and not before" (170). Ambivalence, defined as the disposition both to maintain a stimulus and to cut it off, is easily illustrated by the laughter induced by tickling, a mock-aggression that can be taken in fun only just so long before it yields to fear, discomfort, and tears. Intellectually, if we may put it that way, the baby discriminates between pleasure and pain at that fine point where the one slides into the other.

The ha-ha-has of laughter are produced by a phenomenon unique among respiratory modes. The description is

---

[3] Professor Moses Hadas in class discussion at Columbia College some decades back—in my own college days—gave this unforgettable illustration of the firm distinction between the literal and the figurative: "Children on the beach make sand pies, but they don't eat them."

borrowed by Ambrose from E. L. Lloyd: "In laughter the muscles of inspiration and the muscles of expiration are stimulated *simultaneously.*"[4] Laughter should then not only be seen as a helpless reaction to an event that invites a contradictory response; it is itself compact of contradiction, physiologically speaking. The respiratory apparatus pulls in two opposite directions at once, and we collapse in helplessly *joyous* breathlessness. I emphasize the adjective that sums up the nub of the issue; for why, in good conscience, ought we to deduce pleasurableness from such helplessness if that were not what laughter, in a word, is all about: ambivalence resolved under the sign of the positive?

At the other end of the scale that measures the distance traveled from infancy to maturing, Arthur Schopenhauer ties this joyful embrace of ambiguity to the fact that it lets perception win out over reflection:

> For perception is the original kind of knowledge, inseparable from animal nature, in which everything that gives immediate satisfaction to the will presents itself. It is the medium of the present, of enjoyment and cheerfulness; moreover, it is not associated with any exertion. With thinking the opposite holds good; it is the second power of knowledge, whose exercise always requires some, often considerable, exertion; and it is the conceptions of thinking that are so often opposed to the satisfaction of our immediate desires, since, as the medium of the past, of the future, and of what is serious, they act as the vehicles of our fears, our regrets, and all our cares. It must therefore be delightful for us to see that strict, untiring, and most troublesome governess, our faculty of reason, for once convicted of inadequacy. (2:98)

With a wink to degradation theory, another to play theory, the philosopher of will locates the *fun* of the clash of levels

---

[4] E. L. Lloyd, "The Respiratory Mechanism of Laughter," *Journal of General Psychology* 19:179–89, cited by Ambrose (173, emphasis added).

in an escape from the toils of rationality. That same escape
is trotted out for our benefit, dressed up in the very latest
of twentieth-century intellectual garb this time, by M. J.
Apter and K. C. P. Smith: "An identity synergy represents
an escape, or at least a playful escape, from logic. . . . it
represents an escape from the law of non-contradiction . . .
a particularly strong contradiction since 'not-B' is not just
something different from B but (which is not encompassed
in traditional or modern symbolic logic), something which
is its opposite . . . 'Don't panic' said in a panicky voice"
(98). The case may strike us as badly overgeneralized: not
all comic reversals stand a truth exactly on its head, no
more than they all turn out to substitute the mechanical for
the living. But the message, at any rate, is clear: the joyous
charge packed by the switch is in the nature of a joke
played by our irresponsible, our ebullient selves upon our
sober-sides logical selves trudging glumly in the inescapa-
ble tracks of purposive existence.

One last suggestion we may want to take up in assessing
the binary laughter-triggering gestalt arose in the course of
a dialogue with Gregory Bateson and was made by Lawrence Frank: "The joke may be thought of as involving a
shift between the figure and the ground, where the figure
is altered or the ground is reconstituted or a reversal of
the figure-ground is taking place" (Bateson 7). The hint is
intriguing. E. H. Gombrich, in *Art and Illusion*, shows how
ultimately puzzling is the switch the eye performs on a
trick figure that can be read, alternatively, as a duck looking leftward or a rabbit facing right, the one rendered
invisible by the effort to see the other. The mystery of illusion resides in the impossibility of capturing both views
simultaneously: what *is* there is a function of our apprehension. Is laughter then the apprehension of that inability? Do
we not in the art of raising a laugh voluntarily expose the

single-track character of a mental apparatus incapable of focusing at once on the figure and the ground?

A look at the phenomenon of laughter from the standpoint of what induces it, for all that it locates the risible in a perception of the mind—incongruity—cannot blink the further truth that the "comic" perception is *the perception of a failure of perception.* The mind is briefly taken in. Apparent congruity decomposes into incongruity. The symmetry of a binary configuration collapses into single exposure. What seemed one thing, a club, is really another, a club. The mind's strength—in overcoming the confusion, setting itself straight—exposes the mind's weakness in thus being taken off guard. And we laugh out of both sides of our mouths: Ah, I get it! and how you got me!

The lesson to be drawn, in conclusion, is that of a clash, an agon—the victory handed over to an unlikely/likely party, to a salvo of inhalations of joy and exhalations of grief that resolve into pleasurable helplessness. That the mind both wins and loses in this fight, having backed the wrong horse and then perceived, in an illumination, exactly what made it the wrong horse, may well be—on the intellectual side—the guarantor of an elation that more than meets halfway the euphoria supplied like so much pure oxygen by the emotional presuppositions of laughter.

The Fivefold Way:
A Recapitulation

Le rire . . . impertinent défi jeté à la speculation philosophique.
[Laughter . . . a pert challenge flung at philosophical speculation.]
—Henri Bergson

The three sets of approaches—functional, psychological, intellectualist—that constitute the explanatory field surveyed in the three preceding chapters offer divergent solutions to a problem posed in terms that cross and re-cross common ground. It is that ground I now propose to explore along the lines of a certain number of conclusions that can be pretty effortlessly derived from the cumulative wisdom of our predecessors. They number no more than five—hence this chapter title—and they may be looked upon as the constitutive features of the risible which stand as prolegomena to any comprehensive account of the phenomenon of laughter.

1. In Saulnier's phrase, laughter is an intellectual emotion. Aristotle's claim that alone of all animals man does laugh may be taken as silent acknowledgment of the way a purely physical play of muscles accompanied by audible respiratory pulsation embraces in its genesis both poles of our mental being, the affective and the cerebral. The theoreticians who center their explanation on incongruity (Kant, Hegel, Schopenhauer, Bergson) make abundantly

clear the place of judgment, of the perception of a shift—a break in the train of thought, a "rupture of determinism—in the inception of the laughter response. Paul McGhee goes so far as to posit a correlation between amusement and appropriate intellection: "Humor appreciation," he writes, "is maximized when some optimal amount of cognitive effort is required for comprehension" ("Role of Arousal" 32). A joke that takes too long to work out dissipates in the strain; one that is too childishly obvious fails to take us in.

Others bring out laughter's connection with elation, high spirits, euphoria—all of it conveyed in the noun *mirth*, the adjective *merry*. The word *fun* (which Huizinga pronounces unique to the English language) embraces the whole mood range from childish make-believe to grown-up holiday spirit, from chuckle to guffaw. "Laughter," writes Spinoza in the *Ethics*, "is merely pleasure" (4.65n), and as such the austere sage calls it "in itself good." It must be added that, though he sees mirth as "always good" (4.62), he notes that it "can be conceived more easily than it can be observed" (4.44n). This in virtue of his definition of it as a general elation that "consists in all parts of the body being affected equally," a condition seldom realized in a being whose emotions tend to absorb him in single pursuits (love, greed, ambition). Descartes also speaks of laughter as joy, although he is quick to reckon in an admixture of hatred; and Hobbes's own vivid phrase "sudden glory" speaks of expansiveness and elation.

Freud, moreover, linking wit and humor with a lifting of inhibitions and an economy of psychic expenditure, brings laughter into the heady region of a free spirit, a spirit, that is, that partakes of the spontaneity of that modern version of the poets' Golden Age: childhood. Alexander Bain has already posited the relief it represents from the demands of discipline and decorum, likening it to the schoolchildren's

stampede out of the classroom into the playground. And
James Sully makes the connection with the spirit of play
that rounds out the identification with the effervescence of
our early years. All in all, an emotional tonality is as firmly
attested to as is the cognitive-cerebral dimension, quite
independently of the proven neurological circuit that taps
both the cortex and the hypothalamus.

2. Somewhere along the line most definitions of laughter
bring in the element of surprise: Hobbes's sudden glory,
Descartes's proviso "when that happens unexpectedly
[*inopinément*]," Spencer's gamboling kid breaking in on a
love scene. The explosion of laughter is generally seen as
kindled by the spark of the unexpected. One thinks of
Chaucer's "Miller's Tale," where Alison's anguished cry of
"Water! water!" brings crashing down the carpenter we had
forgotten in his Noah's ark suspended from the roof beam.
It all rushes in on consciousness, grotesquely inappropriate
and yet fully empowered by its own brand of appropriateness to figure in the story at this very moment, reserved for it by a logical powder train of its very own.
Switch, break, rupture: all the key terms of the incongruity
writers smack of punctuality, of an occurrence as near-
instantaneous as the mind can absorb.

Surprise takes on two distinct appearances, that of unexpectedness and that of instantaneity. They deserve separate
consideration.

Aristotle, already cited to the effect, addresses the first
issue, when in *Problems* 2:965a he wonders why it is that no
one tickles himself. His answer, we remember, stresses
unexpectedness as prime in the production of laughter,
which he characterizes as "a sort of surprise and deception." Braced against the onslaught, the ticklee is in some
sense inured to what will come: he cannot be taken unawares. It may be argued, by the way, that tickling oneself
to make oneself laugh would suppose that solitary laughter
is to be looked on as a boon. When it in fact occurs, it is

generally the outcome of a train of thought or the encounter of a moment in narrative, an occurrence in street or home that one hastens to share at the first opportunity. Tickling oneself, when all is said and done, figures most prominently as a derisive offer in response to a failed joke.

A. J. Chapman, in "Humor and Laughter in Social Interaction" makes the point most sweepingly: "Subject laughter is diminished in quantity and quality whenever there is a hint, however subtle, that it is an expected behavior" (McGhee and Goldstein 1:142). Laughter is choked off by the slightest inroad on its spontaneity. Unexpected is also unforeseen: unguarded against, on the one hand; and on the other, unprepared for. Neither positively nor negatively in a state of alert, the subject receives full force an incongruity that shakes her composure. The double take, if compressed enough, leads to the outburst of laughter.

We need only think of the protest "I've heard that one before!" to be reminded how much a fresh impression is the sine qua non of successful comedy. The mind must be tripped into bumping up against one of its own limitations. All we need to be able to say to ourselves to spoil our fun is "I see it coming!" To be taken in at all, the mind must be taken unawares. Surprise, then, is no more than the condition of a pleasurable defeat—pleasurable in part because it lasts no longer than an instant, which invites us to scrutinize that second dimension of the surprise, its instantaneity.

A special case that I had occasion to broach in connection with Dupréel's little water-drop happening allows us the most unimpeded view of the issue. It will be remembered that the drop that slowly formed above, let's say, the nose of the unsuspecting passenger seated under the leak in the streetcar ceiling did so in full view of the fellow passengers, poised to burst out laughing when it hit. The victim alone is taken unawares: *his* surprise is a major ingredient in the fun. We may speak, on the other hand, of a kind of aching certitude on the part of the would-be laughers, fully aware, in fact absolutely certain that the drop will fall, to dramatic effect; uncertain only of the moment. Theirs, as I noted earlier, is pretty much the case of the practical joker who sets up a surprise for another in the expectation of having the laugh on him. Surprise, in either case (both in the passive and in the active sense so far enumerated), is not so much a psychological as a dramatic requirement. It compresses into a single moment the risible contradiction. Kant's intense "expectation reduced to nothing" dissolves, rather, in the joy of a spectacular minireversal. The poise of the unsuspecting victim is instantly shattered by the perpetrator in an instantly reversible mock-catastrophe that loudly proclaims its own factitiousness. No, your bed has not become impenetrable, it has been short-sheeted.[1]

L'arroseur arrosé (The Sprinkler Besprinkled), that earliest of movie shorts of the silent era, makes the case beautifully for the issue of timing versus awareness in the full relishing of a comic episode. The essence of the jest is the maneuver by which the young scamp, who steps on the hose unbeknownst to the gardener, gets the latter to turn the hose on himself in bewilderment over the abrupt cessation of its flow. As he peers intently into the nozzle a pregnant pause develops, filled to bursting with our tipped-off anticipation of what's to come. The explosive release is long enough in coming to have sown a doubt that it would come at all. Our expectation, no longer fully held, sets us up for a surprise at the moment—by then almost despaired of—of its realization. Struck with the harmless force of a splash,[2] the

[1] More drastic practical jokes that inflict more durable pain tip the scales of amusement in the direction of a naked hostility, where laughter turns to vengeful cackle and pleasure in another's pain takes the place of the pleasure of simple merriment, subservient to no alien agenda.
[2] "There is," writes Jean Plaquevent in an "Essai sur le rire chez l'enfant" (An Essay on Laughter in Children), "between life and water a relationship of need to satisfaction that seems so intimate and so essential

gardener suffers a laughable upset, delectable to the degree
that its very harmlessness drowns our scruples—as it lifts
our inhibitions. A climax is reached; inhibitions dissolve
altogether when that piece of mischief gathers its just
deserts in a chase followed by a spanking that gratifies our
sense of completion. The jest is over, life regains homeostasis.

Time, as "timing," "time out," stages the comic surprise.
Like Cinderella's pumpkin coach the comic reversal is forbidden to linger. Over in an instant, that instant in turn is
not itself predictable—except by the comedian, whose art is
compact of timing. Max Eastman's definition of that art,
cited as an epigraph to the preceding chapter, puts it most
crisply: "That is what a joke is—getting somebody going
and then leaving him up in the air" (318). The mind is
thrown off balance by artful timing as surely as ever the
body will be toppled by a treacherous patch of ice. When
Theodore Bickel playfully differentiates a Hungarian from a
Romanian—"Both will sell you their grandmother; but the
Hungarian (*pause*) will deliver!"—even a Hungarian might
be amused by the unexpected dash of surplus skullduggery
that tops the pregnant pause with a double-edged put-
down. Subtract the pause and you are left with no more
than an insult. Tossed at us like a hand grenade, it explodes like one—in its own sweet time. It is a time we put
to use imagining *less* than was to be delivered.

Thus, whether we who are to burst out laughing are
taken unawares by a comic bolt out of the blue, or whether
we are set up and left uncertain only of the time of an
explosively ludicrous resolution, or whether we are given
all the time in the world to burst in at the wrong door, the
element of surprise in one guise or another collapses at

---

that the most irresistible and the most resounding laughter seems to spurt
forth in the child or even in the adult out of the exultation which contact
with it inspires" (154).

least some of our expectations, leaving us prey to helpless laughter.

3. Aristotle's painless deformity combines with Hobbes's sudden glory to situate the comic in the realm of an inconsequential violence, a painless aggression. Both degradation theories and superiority theories make it evident that when we laugh we almost invariably laugh at somebody's or something's expense. More than occasionally the somebody is oneself or, as Hobbes puts it, in place of another's infirmity, "our own formerly." No matter; there is, on the moment, occasion for audible triumph, albeit strictly held in check by the proviso of painlessness.

Painless aggression is aggression legitimated in some sort by its relative mildness, for even in derision it sheds no physical blood. The phrase, in its (unfunny) collocation of near-contraries, calls for attention to both its parts.

Vis comica is the driving energy of comic business that Julius Caesar saw wanting in the art of Terence, which in every other respect he deemed flawless. It is the clearest expression of the aggressive component consecrated in Hobbes's definition. Molière's Alceste, the misanthrope of the play's title who rails at indiscriminate social gush, and promptly falls in love with a tease who soft-soaps every eligible male in town, stamps his foot in rage at the woman he would win. He rants and raves and in good faith thinks himself an exemplary wooer. The wonderful energy of half-lucid self-delusion fills his mouth with more swear words than are to be met with in the rest of Molière's theater. A rather abstract predicament, misanthropy, comes to comic life in the tempestuousness of his temperament. Of the acrobatic antics of the Marx Brothers or the outrageous vulgarity of *Blazing Saddles*[3] the reader scarcely needs to

---

[3] Governor Le Petomane's name in that film, for example, derives from the stage appellation of a celebrated nineteenth-century French music hall performer, Le Pétomane, who executed melodies by modulating his farts (in French, *pets*).

be reminded. Noteworthy in that line, though, is the one comic scene in Chaplin's otherwise maudlin self-glorification film *Limelight*. The imperturbable Keaton, who has the sole comic role in the film, goes on playing as the music sheets become scrambled, as the piano disintegrates. The comedy in this pointedly ignored disaster scene lies in his imperviousness. It makes calamity a joy for the on-looker, saved from consternation by the indestructibility of the clown.[4] Violence reigns unchecked, unnoticed, shorn of consequentiality. We can laugh to our heart's content.

Let us take note, in this context of comedy as a field of force-on-the-loose, of the way the medieval mystery plays came to grief, ending up under official interdict as the devils in them literally walked away with the show, giving the upper hand to the derisive, the prankish, and the ob-scene. Evil, the party of the devil, is, as Blake reminds us, also the party of art, of the poets.[5] Laughter, in its explo-siveness, is an expression of that same—briefly—un-restrained dark energy, heir to the demonic (Harlequin = Erlkönig?),[6] which turns comedy into the unthreatening aspect of anarchy and violence. We must not forget that before the age of romanticism, when Victor Hugo embraced the grotesque—fraternizing with the toad, apotheosizing the rejected—the court dwarf, the natural, the hunchback could be the source of unreflective mirth: an alien defor-mity reaffirming one's own advantages. The shift in sen-sibility makes the hit palpable. Laughter, on the receiving side, packs such a wallop as to leave in no doubt its aggres-sive component.

---

[4] With Keaton, born in a vaudeville family, tossed about on stage as a small child, indestructibility operated as a trademark.

[5] "The reason Milton wrote in fetters when he wrote of Angels & God, and at liberty when of Devils & Hell, is because he was a true Poet, and of the Devil's party without knowing it" (Blake, "Marriage of Heaven and Hell" 182).

[6] See note 3 to Chapter 2.

The flip side of the aggressiveness, we saw, is the prerequisite of mastery, the invulnerability that allows the lowering of one's guard in laughter; a convulsion which, though pleasurable, is temporarily disabling. Ernst Kris observes that little children laugh uproariously at errors they no longer make. Paul McGhee cites D. Horgan to the effect that "humor initiation that takes the form of producing distortion of acquired knowledge may serve to check the accuracy or firmness of one's understanding by testing hypotheses about the nature of that knowledge" (McGhee and Goldstein 1:111). There is method in this apparent madness: laughter, to come into being, has to be sure of its ground. It can also serve to make that ground sure by testing the possibility of laughing about it effectually. Thus what Hobbes and in their turn Bossuet, Baudelaire, Lamennais, and the rest mistake for the essence of laughter, the self's peal of victory over others, may be no more than the condition for laughter: a self utterly secure, for the nonce. Uneasy laughter stands at the antipodes from the laughter of frank amusement. It is utterly incompatible with mirth.

Which is not to say that part of the energy that fuels our laughter is not produced by narrowly averted anxiety. There is the tenseness of the buildup in the joke that threatens us with "not getting" it. There is the barely mastered competence of which Kris speaks that contributes to the loudness of the sudden glory. Such at any rate is the reading Lucien Fabre gives it: "Physically laughter is a release; psychologically, confidence restored [*un rassurement*]" (150).

We come near the borderline of the next issue, that of painlessness. That old dependable, "hoist with his own petard," gives us an entree into the matter. Drawn from the vocabulary of the siege warfare of a bygone age, the age of mines and countermines, it conjures up the satisfying image of the most graphically explicit come-uppance. We

are put in mind of Descartes's proviso that the one laughed
at be justly so derided, that there be a fit between mishap
and evil intent. If, as Nietzsche has it, to laugh is to rejoice
at misfortune with a good conscience, poetic justice, which
so deftly evens the scales of retribution to suit the nature
of the crime, may well be called the morality of laughter.
Caught up in the phrase that signifies that one has tripped
on the very mine he laid, it acts to sweep aside all scruple,
to clear the field of unimpeded mirth.

There is another way in which that vivid locution guides
us into, and out of, the tangle of painlessness. We may, for
instance, take grim satisfaction, but only very moderate
amusement, in the news that a terrorist's bomb blew up in
his own face. To laugh outright we need the sight, evoked
by the phrase in question, of a cartoon figure sailing high
in the air—visible embodiment of a murderous intention
redounding on its author, graceful, economical, irrefutable.
Stylized mayhem lifted clean above the shambles down
below happily removes us from a messy entanglement with
the realities betokened. The great point about pain as it is
entailed in laughter of any description is that it is unreal—
to the one laughing.

This last qualification is not offered in a spirit of cynical
reproof. It literally circumscribes the issue. The issue of
laughter and pain is strictly ascribable to levels of sensibility. Coarse laughter, the laughter of man- and woman-
haters, responds to the wriggles of the tormented, the cries
of their agony, the way the Arkansans in *Huckleberry Finn*
found entertainment "in tying a tin pan to [a dog's] tail and
see him run himself to death." The pain of others, man or
beast, is not real to them; or rather, it spices up an amusement that is predicated on a radical cut-offness, an implaca-
ble hostility. Just as we can work ourselves up to killing the
enemy in war, it is possible to laugh at the antics of those
not of our tribe, whose speech is mere gibberish. Such a

speaker, in Greek, is a *barbaros:* meaningless gabble brands one a barbarian, a being intermediate between man and beast.

Though it is by no means statistically insignificant, the savage laughter that greets cinema atrocities visited in horror films on fiend or on the bespectacled or the luscious victim is not, strictly speaking, the laughter of amusement per se—clear, that is, of pathological or sociopathic entanglement. The fiendish side of our nature must be given its due in the attempt to obtain a broadly authoritative reading of the proviso of painlessness. Repugnant as that acknowledgment may be to the civilized mind, it accounts for the absence of pain that renders feasible the laughter that resounds in the torture chamber. But laughter under less extreme circumstances is more properly the object of our scrutiny.

"C'est une étrange entreprise que celle de faire rire les honnêtes gens," exclaims a character in Molière: it is no simple matter to make the better sort laugh. A variety of distancing devices come into play to insulate the average sensibility (variable as that may be) from whatever pain laughter may inflict. I cannot enumerate them all, but some we have already seen: the stylized mayhem of the cartoons, the balletic rhythmicity of the blows and pratfalls of farce, the indestructibility of Tom and Jerry or of Quixote shedding grinders he never seriously misses and nursing bruises that never cripple. Let us add the ephemeral and purely fictional existence of all characters in the vast oral literature of the joke and the calculated malevolence that earns poetic redress in the hoisting by whatever serves as a petard. Our own sensibility may not let us take the bait. In an ethnic joke, let us say, directed at ourselves or at an outgroup with which we sympathize, hostile intent may shine through for us as distance fails of realization. The point is, we will not laugh. *Vis comica,* if it is allowed to remain merely *vis*, can never in that case become *comica*. Such is the infrangible rule of the game. A nice counterpoise, in closing this section that opened on a note of cruel derision, is Dupréel's assertion regarding our treatment of childish naivete, the *mot d'enfant:* "The harder we laugh at a little child's tottering gait, the greater the urge to give it a big hug" (258).

4. There are all the many ways in which laughter spells freedom. We may reckon in first, since it ties in with the matter just spoken of, the discharge of aggressive energy with so little harm done. Tally as we may the pain (on occasion) inflicted, it bears no comparison to what rage or ill will, let loose on their own, could accomplish. And whether or not we enter into Freud's laborious calculation of psychic economy realized by way of inhibitions lifted in the case of tendentious (that is, aggressive or obscene) wit, we have no trouble unfurling the banner of freedom over laughter that at no cost to ourselves transgresses our taboos.

Robert Torrance elaborates a definition of the comic hero which displays to advantage most of the facets of that freedom which the spontaneity of unforced laughter so irresistibly calls up as of the essence of the comic:

> He is too protean a character to be delimited by any prior definition, since he is forever extemporizing his essence. He does not conform to a single character type at all, be it fool or knave, *eirôn* or *alazôn*, but evades fixed categories of every kind by adopting whatever posture suits his imperious ends. What is constant is the potential or actual antagonism between his ways and those of his world. He is comic (in the root sense of *kômos*, the "revels") primarily by virtue of the festive values that he celebrates and embodies: values of biological life and imaginative freedom, of dogged humanity and belligerent selfhood. (viii)

We are put in mind of slippery, durable, resourceful Odysseus, Torrance's comic hero, who could trick and fib and sweet-talk his way out of cave and cavern and palace hall or courtyard, past siren and nymph and man- and lotoseater, making it home safe from the Trojan War all on his own, when many a doughtier Ajax perished. Naked and alone against a treacherous world, armed with mother wit: can there be a better model of what it is to be free? Polyphemus bellowing that Noman blinded him is proof, if any were wanting, that his opponent, though nominally the hero of an epic, is amply practiced in the ways of comedy.

The freedom *to* exemplified in laughter can also be read as a freedom *from*, as liberation. The various degradation theories (Freud, Bain, Lalo, Souriau) teach us the sense of relief from the realm of value, be it dignity, simple decorum, or adherence to the reality principle or to any set of values whatever (Lalo's polyvalency). Those such as Bossuet and Chesterfield bear witness by their disapproval of a vulgar or profane jocoseness that in the eyes of a bishop or man of high breeding such freedom takes on the aspect of intolerable license. A freedom that gives offense to some at all times, to others on occasion, does no more than live up to its essentially lawless character. I speak here not of political or even moral freedom, which implies some restraints, but of the irresponsible and the gratuitous, which laughter opens up to us for a breathless spell.

The drunkard's pantomime, that key to intercultural hilarity, offers an image of that freedom together with a whiff of its inherent limitations. The lurching drunk widely overshoots his modest goal: a step forward. Next he flails about wildly in a ballet of bodily incompetence, speech slurred, vision blurred—all of it owing to a cause self-inflicted pleasurably, easily remediable, hence safely and delectably risible (in the absence, that is, of spoilsport med-

ical information about what is now viewed as a pathological condition). The spectacle, at all events, is one of limbs
freed from the control of a functioning intelligence, freed to
act on their own, independent of one another and of all
rationally unified purpose. The world of objects appears
equally liberated: lampposts come at him unawares, swing-
ing doors slap him in the behind, an absent mirror is
cunningly impersonated by a fellow duplicating his every
gesture. Fantasy rules the day. Chaplin's normally tight-
fisted millionnaire in *City Lights* turns into a gushing foun-
tain of generous sentiment under the influence of alcohol,
only to swing back to his daytime cold indifference as he
sobers up, leaving Charlie in the lurch. The emotional
seesaw translates on the level of character the disarticu-
lation played out on the bodily level by the comedy of
drunkenness, as it enacts its quasi-Bergsonian scenario of
motion imperfectly mechanized. In a kind of replay of the
fable of the stomach and the limbs in which the limbs seek
to shake visceral tyranny by no longer feeding the stomach
and then starve into submission, the drunken scene exhib-
its the fragility of a liberty that mirrors laughter's own rule
of topsy-turvy. Time once again reasserts its authority over
the realm of the comic. The kind of anarchy let loose by
laughter, in which the diaphragm heaves and the torso
flails out of control, is an instance of maladaptation that
may not exceed its allotted short span. The helplessness of
the drunk, which genuinely endangers his welfare, is the
image of such a reversal—the body having the upper hand
of the mind—unwisely prolonged.

5. Reversal, finally, is indeed the fifth and all-encompassing feature delineated by the explanatory mode center-
ing in descending contrast, binary structure, incongruity.
Reaching all the way back to Kant's expectation reduced to
nothing and, by way of Bain's degradation of an object
possessing dignity, all the way forward to the irrealist's

view that reality itself is for a moment thrown into doubt, a scenario unfolds before our eyes of the brief victory of the lesser over the greater, the worse over the better, the no-account over the weighty. Hegel bemoans the ease with which important and profound thoughts are laughed out of court when they do not conform with the shallow habits of thought of the shallow-minded majority. Schopenhauer gleefully observes the mighty general concept tripped up by the stubborn little particular. For Bergson, summed up in Monro's paraphrase, "any action is potentially comic that calls our attention to the physical in a person" (218), just the put-down effortlessly engineered by the proverbial banana peel.

If we return for a moment to the child's riddle of the fireman, it is as if it offers us an iconic representation of the comic letdown foreseeable in Eastman's "up in the air" quip. "Why does the fireman wear red suspenders?" comes the invitation to puzzle out a detail of sartorial protocol. "To hold up his pants" is a rejoinder that screams in our ear: we were fooled into attending to their vivid color; we missed their humdrum function. The mind's higher function—connecting data, drawing out a pattern, finding a meaning—has been tripped up on the failure to exercise the lower one, simple recognition of the obvious. It picks itself up, smiling. Like the pants, it did not come unhitched.

Kant's formulation, though it is not the first, has the merit of putting it most dramatically. Reduced to nothing, our expectation presents the spectacle of a mighty heave that propels us through an open door—the kind of setup Stan Laurel absentmindedly prepares for the much put upon Oliver Hardy time and again. Joachim Ritter tightens the dialectical screw on the two terms implicit in the contrast: "What plays itself out and is caught up in laughter is the secret connection of nothingness with being. It plays itself out and is caught up, not in the way of exclusionist earnestness, which can do no more than hold it away from itself *as* nothingness, but in such a way that it is shown to inhere in the order which at one and the same time excludes it" (10). What the comic reversal here loses in immediacy it makes up for in subtlety. "Nothing" ceases to be mere absence, it climbs into the bosom of Being, nestles there as if by rights, and in a spirit of mild reproof worthy of Montaigne settles down for good in the realm that spurns it. "We are all wind," writes Montaigne, "and even the wind, more wisely than we, loves to make a noise and move about, and is content with its own functions, without wishing for stability and solidity, qualities that do not belong to it" (trans. Frame 849). Human pride, ontological plenitude are each taken down a peg. They play out for us the schema of a brief reversal in which wind and nothingness strut their short moment at center stage, flaunting their reputed vacuity as plenitude.

The time has now come to reassemble as best I can the pieces of the puzzle. In the next chapter, as I seek to fashion a synthesis that conforms to the five-point agenda set up in these pages, our entree is this fifth and last feature. The microdrama of an unstable reversal lends its frame to a reassembly of those five features. The proviso of painlessness outlined above—since all that does not make for tears may make for laughter—stands guard over the whole assemblage.

CHAPTER SIX

Brief Victory

To be human is to be inherently comic.

—Maurice Charney

J'échappe à la pesanteur en riant. [I escape gravity by laughter.]

—Georges Bataille

Il est peut-être permis par un jour de verglas, . . . de sourire des soudaines et rêveuses gambades des passants. [It may be permissible on a day when the roads are iced over . . . to smile at the sudden and dreamy capers of the passersby.]

—Etienne Souriau

When Plato lets Aristophanes have his say in the *Symposium*, he first pays him off for the ridicule he once poured on Socrates in the *Clouds*, with a bout of hiccups that costs him his turn. The praise of Love he then sets on his lips takes the form, unexpectedly, of a creation myth. In the beginning, Zeus had made humankind spherical; "They were strong also, and had aspiring thoughts. They it was who levied war against the Gods." To bring them to reason, Zeus was obliged to split them in two with a thunderbolt, threatening to split them once more for good measure, "so they shall go about hopping on one leg" (189e–190b). From the time of that amputation dates the invincible nostalgia that the human halves we've turned into endure for the lost other half, whose embrace restores us to blessed sphericity.

When you keep in mind that this odd flight of fancy, this properly *comic* myth breaks in upon a panegyric to Love that opened on the lyrical note "Love, most ancient of the Gods" spoken by the bookish Phaedrus, it is hard not to smile at this first lesson in modesty administered to his fellow drinkers by the poet of the *Clouds* (Socrates was soon to cut their prattle down to size altogether by his depiction of Love's true grandeur as the quest for immortality). By bringing Love down to the level of two bodies melting in an embrace, thus positing its sexual character, Aristophanes does not say by any means all there is to say, but he says what one cannot afford not to say and what the others had left unsaid. All veils are torn asunder: the specious distinction erected by Pausanias to buttress his defense of pederasty, of heavenly and vulgar Aphrodite, is swept aside, the body and its truth not only acknowledged but insisted upon, made double. We are made to experience this corporeality without a pang, so well does the speaker put to use the body's physicality to draw us nearer to it: these half-spheres that languish after a lost plenitude, the proud sphericity turning on its eight limbs at an impressive speed, make up a tableau of a humankind entertainingly distorted, where a joyous physical magnification steps in to fill out a void that was teasingly left gaping.

The philosopher of the Ideal thus appears to have reserved to the comic the function of mouthpiece for the *other* truth, the truth of matter (or, at any rate, of the body). We find in Coleridge a double definition that reinforces the surmise: "The tragic poet idealizes his characters by giving the spiritual part of our nature a more decided preponderance over the animal cravings and impulses than is met with in real life; the comic poet idealizes his characters by making the animal the governing power and the intellectual the mere instrumental" (2:15).[1]

Let us recall as a case in point one of the numerous misadventures of the North American demiurgic Trickster. He willfully and foolishly ingests a bulb that announced, "He who chews me, he will defecate." Soon he is seized by a progressively worsening breaking of wind, a prelude to dire things to come: "The next time he broke wind, he had to hold on to a tree that stood near by. It was a poplar and he held on with all his might yet, nevertheless, even then, his feet flopped up in the air. Again, and for the second time, he held on to it when he broke wind and yet he pulled the tree up by the roots" (Radin 26). It is easy to picture to oneself the shrieks of joy with which the little ones (and their elders) might have greeted such a tale as it unfolded by the campfire. Rabelais, on the other side of the ocean, was to bank on the same brand of overstatement that handed "decided preponderance to the animal" in our nature by way of a celebration of appetite that matched giant bodies with feats of ingestion and excretion of more than proportional volume.

"Man is neither angel nor beast," we read in Pascal, "but it is unfortunately the case that anyone trying to act the angel acts the beast" (trans. Krailsheimer 242). The aphorism delineates the scenario of a comic reversal that sits ready-made in our divided nature, as it is represented in the classical bipolarity of mind and body. The French original, *fait la bête,* carries the more energetic sense of "plays

[1] Perhaps no more than a translation of what August Wilhelm von Schlegel had earlier written: "The earnest ideal consists of the unity and harmonious blending of the sensual man with the mental . . . where the body is wholly pervaded by soul and spiritualized even to a glorious transfiguration. The merry or ludicrous ideal, on the other hand, consists in the perfect harmony and unison of the higher part of our nature, with the animal as the ruling principle. Reason and understanding are represented as the voluntary slaves of the senses" (148–49).

the ass." That the shortest road to making a fool of oneself
is to yield to the temptation of angelism, to take on a sublimity that is not suitable to a being who sweats and on
occasion breaks wind, is comedy enough when baldly
stated. We may see in it the paradigm of comic reversal,
the *fons* and *origo* of all comicality: a being that aspires to
sublimity while solidly compact of flesh and bone. It is a
conclusion with which, in the article "Humour" of the *Encyclopaedia Britannica* (11th ed.), G. K. Chesterton willing-
ly falls in, as he observes that "the very incompatibility
between the sense of human dignity and the perpetual
possibility of incidental indignities produces the primary or
archetypal joke of the old gentleman sitting down suddenly
on the ice." Souriau, in the third epigraph of this chapter,
gives the archetypal joke a decidedly poetic air, as the icy
pavement sends the passers-by into dreamily accelerated
motion. A bit of the same thing is caught by Emerson, who
remarks that "to see a man in a high wind run after a hat
. . is always droll. The relation of the parties is inverted—hat being for the moment master, the bystanders
cheering the hat" (8:169). Cheering for the inanimate pro-
pelled into animation (how un-Bergsonian) lustily takes the
part of the lesser against the greater, or even of the part
against the whole (synecdoche confounded?). It also aligns
the spectators with an uncomplicated physicality to which
the smoothness of ice had already consigned the old gentleman's, well, rump—the least dignified of his bodily
parts.

We are by now familiar with the rule of misrule, the
reign of topsy-turvy. A bloodless revolution takes place,
inverting the familiar landscape, turning our scale of values
on its head. A revolution, that is, firmly wedged into an
interval between two beats of business-as-usual time—be
it a day of carnival, an hour at the circus, the span of a
comedy, the minute it takes a joke to come to the punch

line, or the moment in which we take in a cartoon. Laughter itself, I submit, is such a revolution. For the few gasps it takes us to laugh our heads off, the mind, having been taken in, lets itself be taken over. The lungs and the swaying trunk and the thigh-slapping upper limbs and the tear-befogged eyes have it all their own way, the way of anarchy and discombobulation. Sometimes, of course, we merely signal good-humored defeat with a smile. Only suppose the punch in the punch line had been more forceful; the mind would not just have reeled, it would have briefly come off its moorings, and we should have burst out laughing (as yet we may, from the infectious mirth of a companion). It therefore looks for all the world as if the occasions we give ourselves for laughing (pratfalls, carnival, punch lines, cartoons) mirror rather faithfully in the large the microrevolution that convulses us in hearty laughter: a joyous, a bellowing surrender to the physical, to the mark of our finitude.

The body, shaking loose the restraints of composure, gets its own back on the mind when the mind falters, provided the falter is winked at as pardonable error, a freak induced by surprise, repaired with no pain, rendered palatable by a logic or an appropriateness of its own. The mind connives in its overthrow; the fall is delectable for all the reasons outlined above. The surprise renders it both plausible[2] and permissible; it also numbs, softening the blow. The slip is inconsequential, the shock triggers a harmless explosion. The whole thing is over in a trice, the time it takes to have a good laugh, gone without noticeable fallout. Or, if we broke Mother's favorite ugly vase and all had a good laugh about it, by the time we sweep up the pieces we have sobered up and entered a state that falls outside the purview of comic theory.

---

[2] Recall from Chapter 4 Siegfried J. Schmidt's "das Unerwartete aber doch Bekannte und daher Erkennbare."

Laughter is thus that privileged condition: the *joyous* awareness of our finitude. A friend pointed out to me that, more often than not, it is *my* joyous awareness of *your* finitude. Far be it from me to deny it: Hobbes is not to be denied. Nor is the infinite variety of the comic to be tied to his triumphal chariot. As the animal left free to stumble by the fruitful indeterminacy of his or her programmatic circuitry, (wo)man has evolved a response to intrusive finitude that leaves unimpaired the freedom indeterminacy bestows. We may look upon laughter, therefore, as a freedom exercised upon our own freedom, raising it to the second power, as it were. I spoke of it as anarchic, and indeed it thrives on the brief collapse of our sense of high and low, mind and body, noble and ignoble, turning our scale of values on its head. The best and the worst[3] are permitted to fraternize briefly, for the term of a seizure, in a "letting go" that, though it earned anathemas from the church fathers, restores to the rest of us for the most part some of the resolve needed to face one's daily existence. We need go no farther to remind ourselves of the fact than this passage by D. E. Berlyne from the *Handbook of Social Psychology*:

> Anyone who set out to design a human race without having met any specimens of the existing one might well see no reason why it could not conduct its daily business in deadly earnest. Yet almost all actual human societies appear to expend a great part of their time and energy in playful and humorous pursuits. It may be that all societies have their share of killjoys and spoilsports and prigs, but most of their members seem to prize opportunities for play and laughter and to appreciate other individuals who make appropriate use of them. In our own society, those who devote themselves professionally to the provision of such opportunities are among the most lavishly remunerated and fulsomely idolized. (796)

[3] "Comedy," Rainer Warning defines suggestively, is "negativity turned positive [*Positivierung von Negativität*]" (325).

None but the theoretical mind could be in the least taken aback, I suppose, by the pervasiveness of the risible in human experience, yet some sort of accounting appears necessary for the odd centrality of the gratuitous in human affairs. For all that the functionalists sought to conscript it to some social or even evolutionary use, laughter remains in effect a gratuitous expenditure of breath in response to an inconsequential bit of damage. When we consider, however, that the damage reflects our own ineradicable imperfection, that our laughter arises as we and others bump up against our own limitations, something of the strength that ability implies—to take failure, not as chagrin, but as that purely mental joy we call amusement—impresses itself on us. "Everything human," writes George McFadden, "has a side that is 'all too human', all too personal, and all too mortal. Self-discovery of this side of a person's life can effect a sort of conversion and engender a comic self-knowledge we can literally call 'wholesome'" (101). Finitude is not a great abstraction that falls to our lot by virtue of our being born: it has all the lineaments of our own failure to live up to what we are pleased to imagine ourselves to be. Jessica R. M. Davis puts it wryly: "If farce is tendentious joking, its subversion is limited to a sharing of the open secret that we are all sadly no better than we should be" (394). And that old standby from the Book of Daniel avails B. H. Fussell for a closing homily on the matter: "When we laugh at a baby who tumbles, we laugh at our common feet of clay and our own attempts to rise above them. When we laugh at a grownup who tumbles in his effort to become more erect than we are we laugh because he has forgotten our common feet of clay" (245).

By whatever name you invoke it, finitude inheres in the human condition and the place of laughter is perceived as the kind of cheerful recognition of the fact that keeps us sane, or lucid, or humble—as you choose. The psychiatrist

Harvey Mindess, already cited in Chapter 1 for his tongue-in-cheek assessment of the human animal's preeminent need of laughter ("the only animal who wears clothing, denies himself sex, . . .") neatly encapsulates the therapeutic wisdom: "That is the liberation laughter strives toward: a state of mind keenly aware of its contingency, its relativity, its fallibility" (82). It must be kept in mind, however, that all laughter is not suffused with wisdom. Finitude mocked (in others) is not finitude acknowledged (in ourselves). Mirth partakes of the cheerful recognition that the flesh inclines to (unworthy) creature comforts: "Because thou art virtuous," Sir Toby Belch laughingly reproves the dour Malvolio, "shall there be no more cakes and ale?" (*Twelfth Night* II.iii) But derision is quick to heap scorn on another's stumble, little mindful of commonality in the owning of feet of clay. Though laughter may promote and enhance the flow of cheerful spirits, it seldom can work the miracle of converting to gold the iron of a mean disposition.

Still, the sense of a victory is there. The comic, for Hegel, bespeaks "the infinite lightheartedness and confidence [*Wohlgemuthkeit und Zuversicht*]" of a spirit that is a match for its own contradiction. W. A. Salameh speaks of the comic as the "transformation of the human boundary into the human promise" (85), and Marie Swabey notes that "in the comic judgment in a paradoxical way pleasure takes captive displeasure" (227). Strip the Hobbesian sudden glory of its overload of self-involvement and you have the pure elation of a merry "fix" on the world, capable of wrenching a measure of quiet joy from the facing down of adversity itself. Freud's reading of humor as "the triumph of the ego" may overdramatize a mood that German usage appears to pit singlemindedly against the extremity of one's fate, as gallows humor; but one of the virtues we ascribe to the sense of humor is its creation of a comic perspective from which to maintain one's distance, one's "cool" in the face of an encroaching reality compact of minor and also major menace. The invulnerability that is the other face of comic energy takes the form, in humor, of a deliberate creation. Joking in the face of danger is a way of distancing oneself physically, of gaining a purchase on the ambient hostility, of treating it as harmless by fiat. The comic being, as we have seen, a brief suspension of belief in the reality of the real, lifting from our shoulders the ever-present weight of seriousness—Lorenz's *tierischer Ernst*—when exercised under circumstances that appear to forbid such a relaxation turns into a show of force on the part of one truly self-confident. The studied nonchalance of Castiglione's Renaissance courtier, his *sprezzatura*, offers a parallel to that spirit of lighthearted consignment of the disastrous to the mild and mundane that presides over British humor. In the darkest days of the Second World War, when the nation that coined *Nacht und Nebel* (Night and Fog) had unleashed the full horror of air warfare on the sprawl of a vast and populous city, London was plastered with signs on bomb-damaged shop windows proclaiming "Open as usual." One particularly devastated store, with hardly one wall left standing, jauntily worded its sign "More open than usual." Going down not with a guffaw but with a merry twinkle, surely.

The prankishness of the young testifies no less to a spirit of overcoming than the laughter in the teeth of life's perilousness. D. Horgan observed her 16-month-old daughter, having learned the word "shoe," poking her foot through the armhole of her nightgown, exclaiming "shoe" with shrieks of laughter (McGhee and Goldstein 1:110). The relentless pressure of humanization, in the form, mostly, of language acquisition, is not to be borne without the occasional flareup of a willful violation of the rules, turning them briefly against themselves to gain a permissible leverage that spells impunity. Tiny Kelly (that is her name) is on to us, and she knows enough to play our game with a nimbleness that lets her steal a march on the didactic enterprise. The insurgent spirit of comedy in her takes the form of an inventiveness that shakes lose the categories of the literal-minded, frees the shoe from its leather envelope to become pure foot-fitting concept (in defiance of Schopenhauer's dictum on the particular tripping up the conceptual). If we measure the respective power and size of the two contestants, the babe-in-arms and the consensus of the English-speaking world, on the semantic latitude granted the monosyllable *shoe*, it is hard not to see in young Kelly a David bringing down (unharmed) our Goliath.

The stand-up comedian, at the other end of a scale measuring age or sophistication, trades, for her part, on the dubious, the threatening, the unspeakable—holding chaos at bay by dabbling in it nonchalantly. Cruelty, vileness, the ugly, and the insensitive are held up to us in her patter only to be put down amid our laughter. She is the artist of Fabre's view of the comic, as *désarroi-rassurement*, moving us from upset to reassurance. Mayhem is verbalized, transposed from the realm of fracas and hurt to the respite of mere words, just as Jerry the cat, flattened to a board in an animated cartoon, is permitted in the next frame to resume his evil ways undeterred. Seymour and Rhoda Fisher, in their investigation of personality and psychopathology in the comic, remark on "a preoccupation with morality and a sense of obligation to do good" (57) as a prominent feature of their subjects' lives. Like the jester of yore they stand guard, with acrobatic nimbleness, over the impermissible. Theirs the mission to face up to the unbearable, rendering it bearable for us as well as for themselves. Woody Allen obsessively puts down his (our) puniness, dressing it up in a fantasy of bragadoccio: scrawny and owlishly bespectacled he proclaims himself an animal of heedless sensuality. David Brenner throws in a casual reference to Three Mile Island, seat of the near-disaster at a nuclear reactor plant, reminding us that it came close to earning for itself the name Two Inch Island. Evil trips off the tongue both glowering and diminished, a lifelong humiliation transmutes to amusement. The Fishers, in *Pretend the World Is Funny and Forever*, bring out how Chaplin's "costume speaks of disproportion, contradiction, and yet of an ease with object size gone awry" (90). The clown's timeless inheritance of baggy pants and tiny bowler hat speaks with eloquent muteness of a being who rises effortlessly superior to shabbiness and bedragglement, borne aloft on the wave upon wave of laughter he earns himself by ignoring his rags, by turning them into the banner of his acrobatic elegance, hooking the silly cane around the throat of a hulking adversary, shrugging off buffets, traipsing unbowed into the sunset.

When Molière, on the other hand, makes it known that the business of wringing laughter from our betters is no simple matter, *les honnêtes gens* he has in mind represent no less than the social and political elite of the age, the court aristocracy, men and women who pride themselves on self-control, easy mastery of the social graces, tact, finesse, and an innate elegance. To shake the composure of a king, for Louis XIV was Molière's enthusiastic patron, the *vis comica* had to create for itself targets both plausible and fully deserving of its blows, lest conscience rebel or taste receive offense. The rogues' gallery of life's excesses, its fops, its misers, its frauds, and its bullies, had to be represented faithfully enough to display human error and vice in their risible nakedness. Facile jokes at the expense of braggarts and gluttons made way for the depiction of a malfeasance nearer the mark of daily existence, while to the joy of seeing rascals undone was superadded the sense of the justice of their undoing.

Comedy might also be characterized as an amused (rather than an indignant) recognition of the skullduggery universally prevalent among humankind. We rejoice in the laughing rogue's putting down of the unlaughing one, be the former Till Eulenspiegel, Reinhard the Fox, or Rabelais's Panurge. Equally we rejoice in the unlicensed rogue defeating the rogue in office, be he Molière's Scapin or Thomas Mann's Felix Krull, confidence man. And, of course, from the days of Menander to the novels of Wodehouse we equally rejoice in that perdurable myth of comedy-cum-romance—the victory of youth over age, with an assist from an agile, a conniving underling, to the tune that never loses its tang, the music of desire.

Freud's *Witz*, to look at another point of the horizon of comedy, the bon mot, the stroke of wit, unveils the treachery of linguistic usage. We are set up by the shape of a locution to expect one thing and made to receive another. In "He is in his anecdotage" (Freud's English example), a common disyllable *dot-age* favors the engrafting of a characterization upon a cliche, lending it renewed power of disparagement. Invention takes the place of weary resignation (all these anecdotes!), a sprightly creation perks us up: *le mécanique* is made to yield *du vivant*. We have been translated unexpectedly from the realm of the reportorial to that of the creative, as language reanimates our dull expectation, projects us, unbidden, to a higher sphere. Like the fellow who slips on a banana peel, we simultaneously feel the weight of our body (here, mental routine) and its sudden projectile capability, having been hurled into the air by an agency beneath notice—yet another chapter in the triumph of the lesser over the greater.

Victory is not all in the hands of the wits and the rogues, however. A striking image recurs under the pen of two writers of widely divergent inclination. In William Willeford's *The Fool and His Scepter* we read, "The fool as

moral agent—as in other respects—is like the child's toy
called in German Stehaufmännchen . . . and in English
tumbler or roly-poly. . . . The toy is not in conflict with
the 'bad' person who hits it. It simply reacts with simplicity . . . according to inviolable physical laws and without expending energy of its own" (115). Marie Swabey
writes, for her part, "Comic characters remind us of those
toy weighted figures beloved of children that right themselves after every upset with a resilient upswing suggesting
a buoyant affirmation of life" (136–37). It is all grist to the
mill of George McFadden's more sweeping assessment:
"The essence of the comic . . . is founded in a being that
shows the power of continuing as itself, substantially un-
changed, while overcoming a force or forces that would
substantially alter it" (12). What each author salutes in this
figure of unassuming inalterability is a kind of passive resistance that is the strength of the weak. By a sort of jujitsu
the fool enlists the power of the blow to stun the aggressor
with an unlooked-for return on his exertion. Swabey exalts
perdurability into affirmation; McFadden, standing Bergson
on his head, makes sheer inertial being-there the fundamental victory of comedy. The fool is forever, as is the
clown: a low profile, in each case, a humble station,
purchase for them that comic invulnerability that is one of
the conditions of laughter. Resilience, in them, turns hand
springs on its pursuers, as is the way of Chaplin: with
Keaton, in Gerald Mast's happy phrase, it turns "his moving body into a small piece of elastic granite" (130).

   To call another's bluff, to prick her balloon, or even to
exclaim, as did the child in Andersen's tale, that the emper-
or is naked, is a not unrelated form of the ubiquitous comic
turn, getting the better of one's supposed betters. Max
Eastman gives it a quite elaborated justification: "Our lives
in all departments consist so largely of the cultivation of
insubstantial pretenses and amenities, the feeding of thin
glamours—of posturing and pretending, sometimes honor-

ably, sometimes with self-contempt—that almost any perfectly candid speech about anything contains an element of
release" (272). Structured as a deflation, the airiness of our
vanities exposed by the sharp edge of that monosyllable,
speech, Eastman's grandiose periodic sentence mimics what
it would convey: plain Jane cutting through pretense at a
pleasurable stroke.

A masterpiece in this game of artful deflation, of the
grand shown up in the light of either the silly or the
tawdry (take your pick), is Santayana's joke on Hegel,
perpetrated with all the tongue-in-cheek gravity of a philosophical argument. I cannot resist quoting it in full:

> Suppose I abstract a coin from another man's pocket: it is easily
> proved by Hegel's logic that such an abstraction is a mere
> appearance. Coins cannot exist as coins except as pocketed and
> owned; at the same time they imply an essential tendency to
> pass into the pockets of other men: for a coin that could not
> issue from the pocket would be a coin in name only, and not in
> function. When it actually passes from one man's pocket into
> another's, this circumstance, far from justifying us in thinking
> the coin a separable thing, shows that all men's pockets (when
> not empty and therefore, in function, not pockets at all) are
> intrinsically related and, in a higher sense, one and the same
> purse. Therefore, we may conclude, it was not the sly transfer-
> ence of the coin from my neighbour's pocket into mine that
> was the wrongful abstraction, but only the false supposition
> that if the coin was his it was not, by right of eminent domain,
> mine also. A man, in so far as he is the possessor of a pocket,
> and all pockets, in so far as there is transferable coin in them,
> are one pocket together. In this way we avoid false abstraction
> by proving that everything is abstract. (206)

In the vein of absolute deflation, or of deflation of the Absolute, little remains to be told that comes up to this deft
exercise.

Laughter as the euphoric acknowledgment of finitude,

the comic as the ubiquitous exercise of the faculty of turning the tables on what we value, or fear, or feel oppressed by, celebrate together the safely short-lived victory of the lesser over the greater, and even of the worse over the better, for the recreation of our spirits by a timely holiday from all earnest pursuits. For a blessed moment we enter a godlike impunity, our foes disarmed, our fears stilled, our aggressions rendered permissible by a mutual compact of blamelessness. The mind deliciously surrenders to an admission of defeat, wrung from it by surprise, while the body is given leave to abandon itself to an orgy of heaves and flailings for an interval calculated to remain inconsequential. Built into the nervous system of *Homo sapiens*— the animal that climbed to the top of the heap of animate existence by an ability to gather knowledge that earned it well-nigh absolute control over all the resources of the planet—the capacity to let go of that control for a spell, time and again (up to 150 times an hour!), testifies to a saving elasticity that shores up mastery in the act of mocking it. The animal that laughs may yet escape entrapment in its own achievement.

No nearer approach exists, in human affairs, to a claim of partaking in the sublime than the august ceremonial of religion. The feast days that in the liturgy of the medieval church signaled a radical inversion akin to that of laughter set the hierarchy rudely on its head on Holy Innocents' Day by the appointment of a boy bishop. On the Feast of Fools, the lower clergy elected a Lord of Misrule. On the Feast of Asses, "as a festival commemorating Mary's flight into Egypt, an ass was ridden into the sanctuary by a young girl carrying an infant boy. With the ass and the riders standing beside the altar, a mass was sung in dog-Latin rhyme, with the priest and congregation braying the refrain: 'Haw, Sir Ass, he-haw'" (Hyers 18).[4]

---

[4] Anne Witte's dissertation, "A Study of the Feast of the Ass in Thirteenth-Century France," soon to be defended in the French Doctoral

What better way to salute our joyously humbling kinship with brute creation than a unison achieved in song with the ass, that patient, much-maligned, unmusical beast, emblem of human thickheadedness? It is thus invited to stand for the truth that in the kingdom of laughter the first shall indeed be the last, that he who would truly bless shall on occasion bray. Is that not small price to pay for the gift of seeing oneself on occasion as others see us, chuckling where we might have good cause to quail? For the humility religion enjoins upon us, laughter effortlessly bestows it, unthanked and largely unremarked.

Program of the University of the City of New York (CUNY), seriously undermines the traditional case for tomfoolery assumed by Hyers and his otherwise authoritative sources. The ass's bray may not have sounded in church in the thirteenth century; it resounded unequivocally, however, in that centuries-old misreading (which goes back to Ducange's *Glossarium*.)

CHAPTER SEVEN

Art

Der Witz wird gemacht, die Komik wird gefunden. [A joke is
something made; the comic something found.]

—Sigmund Freud

In tragoedia fugienda vita, in comoedia capessenda. [In tragedy life
is a thing to be fled. In comedy it is something to hold.]

—Evanthius

That natural portrait of human Folly and Frailty of which all are
judges, because all have sat for the picture.

—Oliver Goldsmith

The soul of comedy is the brain.

—Gerald Mast

Freud's relegation of the comic to the realm of objet
trouvé notwithstanding, occasions for laughter are mostly
the products of human ingenuity—jokes, puns, vaudeville
acts, stage comedies, cartoons—and as such fall within the
domain of art. Grins, smiles, titters, chuckles, guffaws,
hoots, and belly laughs form a series that gives but a feeble
approximation of the infinite variety of the risible fare at
our disposal. Babes in arms and toothless crones, men of
war and lovers of peace, the idle and the busy, the rich and
the poor, the learned and the unlearned all laugh, and
matter is made up that suits most moods and most palates.

A survey of the laughable need aim at no more than a sampling, therefore, as no more can be looked for realistically. It is meet that we test our views against a suitable range of recognizable comic occurrences: the medley that follows is a stab in that direction.

Helen Bacon offers a helpful text for getting us under way: "Both comedy and tragedy center around man's relation to error. The unacknowledged error is the cause of a misplaced complacency which is comic, the acknowledgement of error, with its shattering of complacency and illusion, is in essence a recognition scene, which is the heart of tragedy" (430).

Error, the very name of our frailty, both moral and intellectual, is nowhere so entertainingly inscribed as in the condition that gave Shakespeare a title for *The Comedy of Errors*. Twins are nature's own enigmatic little joke, *lusus naturae*. Pascal, in the epigraph to Chapter 4, seizes on the immediacy of the effect attained: "Two faces are alike; neither is funny by itself, but side by side their likeness makes us laugh" (trans. Krailsheimer 34). And what if they should be, not alike merely, but identical?

Comedy has still a better use for that uncanny reduplication, laughable in itself: permutation. One Antipholus taken for another, Zeus in bed with Alcmena in the guise of her husband Amphitryo, Sebastian married in place of Viola all sow short-term dismay and soon dissipated consternation. Everything is unaccountably taken from the one and just as unaccountably lavished upon the other. A strongarm Mercury, in Plautus (and Molière) strips the slave Sosias, whom he so supernaturally impersonates, not only of his job but of his name, while a drubbing falls on the shoulders of the one Dromo that had been earned by the other. Blissfully the one Antipholus drinks in an unsought good fortune, while the other is driven from hearth and home: we the godlike spectators are privy to the whole transaction, their partial error making up our undivided apprehension. The triumph of finitude, in a comedy of this type, as in the practical joke with which it has affinity, is all for the benefit of a third party, sitting in sovereign detachment from the imbroglio. The joke is on *them*, but the play ticks off sufficient grounds of kinship between us and them to keep us amused at a common fragility. A fate so symmetrically/contradictorily divided mocks at that grandiose property, man's fate, providing deft demolition of human self-importance.

A great leap backward along the evolutionary scale of dramatic sophistication takes us to the nursery room, where a game practiced far and wide receives in English the appellation peekaboo. It too centers on a carefully nurtured error. Covering her eyes with her hands, the mother mimics a mildly frantic search. "Where is baby?" she intones, "where could baby have gone to?" facing exactly in baby's direction. "There she is!" she exclaims triumphantly, uncovering her eyes before excitement can make way for anxiety. Gurgles and peals of appreciation ensue on the part of the foundling. The drama is artless but it thrives on a heady emotional mixture. Mother's temporary disarray is a boon, a threat, and a victory to its tiny observer. It is a boon in the form of heightened attention to baby's person, dramatic confirmation of its importance for Mother—which is in fact the point of the game. It is a threat, obviously; for what if her blindness is incurable? what if I'm lost sight of for good? the vital nurturant connection broken? (words only too obviously put in the babe's mouth). It is a victory of the little one over the big lumbering mock-incompetent one on two counts: baby never is lost in its own eyes, lying snugly in its cradle right in front of her; and, to noisy rejoicing, it is soon found again, as Mother regains her sight. We have here a mixture, then, of sudden glory and euphoria—the victory of the lesser over the greater, the spectator given full benefit of a superior vantage point, once more, that insulates her to a degree from the error portrayed.

While we abide amid childish pleasures, it may not be amiss to play a game of a quite different sort and explore a purely phonetic recreation, in line with H. L. Mencken's caustic observation that the sound *k* in a proper name afforded peculiar joy to the American moron. Let us take the case of *Kalamazoo:* what makes it, to some, a funny-sounding name? Three short steps in [a] led in by three alphabetically consecutive consonants [k, l, m], occlusive, liquid, labial, respectively (that is, progressing from posterior to anterior buccal cavity), act as a ladder, rising to the highest note in the English register [u], which slides in on us over the glistening parquet of the soft sibilant [z], puckering up the mouth in gentle mockery of itself. Quite a performance, in other words: the alphabet showing off, calling attention to the humble purveyor of our communicative means in a display more acrobatic than seductive. Where poetry foregrounds the music of the language, luring the ear with euphony, the drum-and-fife of *Kalamazoo* alerts the critical sense to playful incongruity. The mind is passingly distracted from its higher obligation to attend to the sense, a city of southwestern Michigan, pop. 82,000.

The unconscious comedy of learned discourse, of which a couple of examples came into view on the way to these pages, may find itself in place here. In an essay coauthored by a cohort of researchers, "Ethnic Humour as a Function of Social-Normative Incongruity and Ego-Involvement," we read that, in a given experiment, "the cow nonanticonforms" (Issner et al. 281). With an equally straight face Arthur Pickard-Cambridge, in *Dithyramb, Tragedy, and Comedy,* reels off on page 196 that remarkable bit of obscurantism, "epirrhematic syzygy"—in plain English, a pairing of scenes. End of learned parenthesis.

Freud credits the child's free play with the sounds of the

language as the source of the pleasure we take in verbal humor. A no less fertile mode of nursery school entertainment is the shrieking delight taken in the simple fact of dropping one's knickers (preferably, in the case of the other fellow, involuntarily). "Children," writes M. L. Apte in bland, faintly comical "scientific" understatement, "are generally curious about their bodies and the elimination of waste" (92). At the juncture of nature and culture the naked baby finds itself (outside aboriginal conditions) an object of a mysterious (because culturally motivated) solicitude touching two anatomical properties: the body is clad, the waste disposed of. Such are the imperatives of culture, in varying degrees of rigor and alarm. The comic open secret: beneath my underthings there is to be found a body, complete with "secret" parts, and it both shits and pisses. Though this "news" is no longer quite news as we grow older, it can still be made to function as novelty: witness the respectable body of jokes of which such a disclosure furnishes the punch line.

Writing in the final decade of the twentieth century, I enjoy the freedom (at least I take it so) of naming these functions by their more explosive onomatopoeic names, a breach of decorum for the sake of comic expressiveness which I expect my readers to forgive. Not so long ago such an expectation would have been thought worse than fatuous, such a liberty licentious. It is hard therefore to gainsay that part at least of the comic force of such usage derives from the lifting of inhibitions; that the body excremental, in other words, operates in the literature of scatology that rather operatic maneuver dear to the heart of today's hermeneutes, the return of the repressed.

Be that as it may, the gingerly dance of common parlance around that area of experience parallels amusingly the understandable reluctance most of us feel at entering into close contact with the matter in hand. One clan's euphemism is the other's amused disbelief: whether you pee, pi-pi, take a leak, pass water, do number one, or, less creditably still, urinate or even micturate . . . there is no right way, safe from derision, to name the activity that takes you to the privy (in Spanish, tellingly, *retretas*) not once but several times daily, every last day of your life. The squeamish reader may squirm (note the expressive [skw] formations) at what may be judged excessive lengths devoted to the least palatable of the comic turns our body forces upon us, but short of the sexual (whose turn is to come) the excretory is one of the most imposing reservoirs of laughing matter our nature hands to us (in justification of Freud's *wird gefunden*). The puritanical revulsion that washed over Europe in the wake of the combined excesses of the French Revolution and the aristocratic decadence that had invited it has tended to sweep these manifestations underground, but one need only recall Sancho, after the ingestion of Fierabras's balm, "discharging at both ends" to realize that the high culture was not always so dainty. Voltaire's Candide, spanked to music (*fessé en cadence*) in the course of an auto-da-fé, testifies to the comic force of an apt reference to the rump. Blows to that fleshy part of our anatomy represent a harmless indignity, redolent of puerility and excretion. Administered in cadence, they wed euphoria and humble physicality, with little of dire consequence. An image is called up of a chorus of high-kickers lined up toe to rump, something like the *cordax* of the beginnings of Greek comedy.

In point of fact the comedy of the body's shameless all-encompassing physicality, of its huge appetites and correspondingly vast outpourings at the nether conduits, has a name: it is Rabelaisian. Uncloistered monk, Hellenist, physician, polymath, author of giants' chronicles in the popular taste that are crammed with classical erudition, that burst at the seams with encyclopedic enumerations of unparal-

leled earthiness and rare virulence, directed impartially
at Sorbonne theologians and unlettered friars, François
Rabelais is the arch-representative of that Renaissance cult
of abundance, of excess, that *copia* emblematized, as
Terence Cave reminds us, by the horn of plenty.[1] The infant Gargantua, after consuming the milk of "seventeen-
thousand-nine-hundred-thirteen cows," is seen happily to
"rock in his cradle, dandling his head, monochordizing
with his fingers, and barytoning with his behind." Later
on, "from the age of five years,"

> he wallowed in the mud, smudged his nose, dirtied his face,
> ran his shoes over at the heels, frequently caught flies with his
> mouth, and liked to chase the butterflies of his father's realms.
> He pissed over his shoes, shit in his shirt, wiped his nose on
> his sleeve, dropped snot in his soup, and paddled around
> everywhere. (trans. Putnam 71–72, 79)

The enumeration spreads over two pages. Once grown up
to man's estate, after an education that ranged from the
mastery of all ancient tongues to the honing of the talents
of a remount officer, he fought the Cakepeddlers' War,
drowning opponents in a flood of urine, picking canon
balls out of his hair. As comic appetite made way for comic
mayhem, the mettlesome monk John Hackem shone forth,
who in defence of the abbey close laid on with the staff of
the cross to such remarkably good effect:

> He beat in some of their heads, broke the arms and legs of
> others, unjointed the neck-vertebrae of still others, dislocated
> the loins of others still, bashed in their noses, gouged out their
> eyes, split their jaw-bones, sunk their teeth in their chops,
> crushed their shoulder-blades, mangled their shins, unhinged
> their hips, and hewed to pieces their forearms and shanks. . . .

[1] Terence Cave, *The Cornucopian Text: Problems of Writing in the French
Renaissance* (Oxford: Clarendon, 1979).

If any tried to save themselves by flight, he stove their heads
into bits, by way of the lambdoid suture. . . .
   Some died without speaking, others spoke without dying;
some died while they spoke, others spoke while they died.
(148–49)

In recompense of such heroic carnage, salvific of the year's
wine grape harvest, and of other such high feats, Gargantua granted him at war's end the abbey of Thélème, a
cloister without walls whose motto was "Do what you
will." Pantagruel, son and successor of Gargantua, would
in his own accomplished young manhood befriend that
paragon of unprincipled scoundrels, Panurge, one of whose
unforgettable pranks it is to smear the genitals of a bitch in
heat, chopped fine, on the train of a lady who scorns his
advances, to see the unfortunate woman mounted and
bepissed by all the male dogs in Paris.
   Rabelais, understandably, is not to everyone's taste. The
fare is gross, sometimes outrageous, at all times robust,
more so than we may care to stomach. The wonder is that
he could exist at all in a language that within a century
was to be pared down to the requirements of neoclassical
understatement. Yet overstate he does happily, exuberantly,
uninhibitedly, in an orgy of unbounded affirmation. That
religion of excess will foster, or at all events authorize, later
developments in the literature of comic outrageousness. We
owe to Rabelais's example Alfred Jarry's ferocious creation
Ubu roi (1896), that schoolboy's prank grown to the dimensions of a presurrealist masterpiece, forerunner of the
theater of the absurd. Endowed with the sensibility of a
bloody-minded puppet, a Punch on the rampage, the grotesque Père Ubu, egged on by his Lady Macbeth of a mate,
Mère Ubu, drenches the throne of a mythical Poland in
blood and booty in the manner of a naked id, to the tune
of his favorite oath, "by my green tallow-candle," punctuat-

ing his misdeeds with his tradename obscenity, the opening word of the play, "Merdre!" (Shittr! in Barbara Wright's New Directions translation). Rewriting language with the same cheerful abandon as he replenishes his phynances with the confiscated wealth of his nobles, given over to execution en masse, Ubu, whose cowardice in defeat fully matches his bloodthirstiness in victory, displays that cartoon-like simplification of motives and acceleration of pace that presents to our half-amused, half-horrified recognition the amplified tableau of the misdeeds of what, over much of the globe, passes for government.

The comedy of outrageousness, knowingly trampling over all so-called civilized restraints, mangling flesh and crunching bones with high cannibalistic relish, today flourishes under the improbably lettered banner of the Monty Python Flying Circus. In both television singles and full-length moving picture features, under the sign of an animated cartoon that squashes talking heads and spews bodies out of gaping maws, a merry crew of earnest bunglers take off on all that is left today that is either sacred or unmentionable, ranging from BBC solemnities to limp-wristed effeminacy, from childbirth to the Crucifixion. The relentless idiocy in which the media smothers us to the tune of "all is well," while it simultaneously delights in parading before us all that is horrifyingly wrong, from napalm-drenched children to the latest grisly dismembering or billion-dollar swindle, could not be more effectively exposed for what it is—insanity posing as sanity—than by the sight of a surgeon reaching into the liver of a howling patient while a song is crooned to the heavens about the wonders of the cosmos. Hyperbolic folly calls for a cure drawn from the arsenal of hyperbole, it would seem.

Pairing is a standard resource of comedy. One thinks of Laurel and Hardy, Mutt and Jeff, Don Giovanni and Leporello. One thinks first and foremost of Don Quixote and

Sancho Panza, the archetypal pair, one tall and thin, thinking thin and elevated thoughts, the other short and squat,
thinking thoughts as down-to-earth as his own stature
suggests. Contrast is a powerful agent of the comic double
take, one mode of discourse both meeting and somehow
eluding the other at all points. The play of size by itself
creates something of a visual gag. Juxtapose an elephant
and a mouse, the one scurrying by the other's path; you
will amuse perhaps no more than a three-year old. Perch
the mouse provocatively on the elephant's occipital bone;
the diminutive size of the one operates as a silent com-
ment, or so it seems, on the extravagant bulk of the
other— human stature filling in as the hidden middle term,
the implicit norm so laughingly violated at either end of the
spectrum.

Perennially dependable, a pair that can be found to
lodge exclusively in the halls of comic theory is that of wit
versus humor. An effort is generally made to define the
one as not being the other. Mind and heart offer a convenient opposition on which to hang the contrast. In H. W.
Fowler's "Classification of the Ludicrous" (*English Usage*)
they fare as follows:

	Motive or aim	Province	Method or means	Audience
Humor	Discovery	Human nature	Observation	The sympathetic
Wit	Throwing light	Ideas	Surprise	The intelligent

Voltaire's saying of the author of a poem on the pox "there
goes an author deep in his subject [*bien plein de son sujet*]"
makes crystal clear why wit in French is referred to in the
likeness of a spear or an arrow: un *trait* d'esprit. The
French language, so rich in homonyms, lends itself so well
to the game of wit that we have tended to reserve the faculty to that nation. The Viennese lag not all that far behind,
as Freud demonstrates from his citations of a high person-

age he calls N who on the occasion of the resignation of an
obtuse minister of agriculture quipped, "Like Cincinnatus,
he returned *before* the plough." Brevity is not fortuitously
presented as the soul of wit: the means are so fine, the
end so swift, the switch thrown so unexpectedly that the
aggression earns impunity from the art with which it
throws us into confusion. Indignation's hand (suppos-
ing ourselves the target of so deft a stroke) is stayed by
admiration.

A last example I cannot resist. At the time that a con-
servative Supreme Court threatened to throw out his New
Deal legislation, Roosevelt contemplated a move to pack it
with a few extra judges. The court saw the light and ruled
affirmatively at the next opportunity. An anonymous genius of a headline writer captioned the event "A Switch in
Time Saves Nine." The *switch* is triply apt. It presides over
the meeting of a proverb ("A stitch in time saves nine"), of
a politic turnaround (nine judges reading the New Deal
writing on the wall), of its own sleight of hand (in a switch,
sneaking *w* in the place of *t*). It exploits, moreover, a
humorous conjunction, nine judges on the Supreme Court,
nine stitches in the proverbial count, putting it to pregnant
use in characterizing a judicial/judicious decision sup-
posedly arrived at objectively. More than a grain of malice
flavors the tour de force. Aptness, compression, an unexpected juxtaposition that strikes a spark, its illumination
not unmingled with hellish glee, such are the makings of a
bon mot. Mind surely has more to do with it than heart, in
deference to our fourth epigraph: "The soul of comedy is
the brain."

In humor, the finitude of the human condition is more
apt to be endured, even to be shared with a rueful smile,
than to be inflicted. We have seen how the German version
of the thing soon veers into the dire. Maurice Charney
(*Comedy: New Perspectives* 32) cites in this regard an old

German saying: *Humor ist, wenn man trotzdem lacht* (call it humor when you laugh just the same). The English variety appears to hark back to the four humours of Renaissance medicine-cum-characterology: the sanguine, the choleric, the melancholy, and the phlegmatic. The theater of Ben Jonson in particular opted for a comic of eccentricity, of everyman in his humour, that is, indefectibly wed to his own peculiar ways. Horace Walpole was to give a humorous etiology to this prevalence of humours: "In this nation we have certainly more characters than are seen in any other, owing perhaps to two causes, our liberty and the uncertainty of our climate" (cited in Wimsatt 202). A figure that for me quite sums up that particular tradition is Lewis Carroll's White Knight, who crashes his way across Looking Glass land wrapped in countless ingenious devices "of [his] own invention," none of which help him do so much as stay upright on his horse. The gentle woebegone everhopeful demeanor matching the drooping moustache bespeaks a being bloodied but unbowed by the hazily acknowledged unkindness of fate. Humor in this mode falls in with finitude only too readily.

Gentle, and not-so-gentle, kidding marks the American brand of humor, whose rougher texture reflects the pioneering experience. A strain of sly indirection can be detected, heir to a close-mouthed countryside tradition. Max Eastman cites a particularly devastating bit of Mark Twain ellipsis: "A traveler would have missed the noon train yesterday, had he not stepped on a peach pit at the head of the depot stairs" (181). The laconic account is redolent of the desolation of a sparsely populated landscape, where a man missing his footing and hurtling down a flight of stairs is drama enough to relish through the sparsest of retellings. The mind's eye is invited to take it all in, luxuriating in the silent commotion.

A passage in Twain that invariably brings me to an inner chuckle is Huck's recounting to himself of a Sunday in church alongside the piously murderous Grangerfords:

> It was pretty ornery preaching—all about brotherly love, and suchlike tiresomeness; but everybody said it was a good sermon, and they all talked it over going home, and had such a powerful lot to say about faith and good works and free grace and preforeordination, and I don't know what all, that it did seem to me to be one of the roughest Sundays I had run across yet. (109)

Ironies abound: brother love is a theme taken up enthusiastically by a clan that is just about to engage in lethal confrontation with a neighboring family over a Romeo-and-Juliet elopement; these same gun-happy model Americans expound theology with a will, exulting in good works on the eve of a massacre; Huck alone resists preachment, he whose heart is pure of murderous, or even unloving, thoughts. But the humor of it lies in the heartfelt distaste of the simple in heart, of Huck, for the poisonous verbiage on which the others feed, and which he knows no better way of characterizing than "tiresomeness" and "of the roughest": a dismissal no less apt for being pungently, rather than indignantly, put. Huck's innate goodness and rectitude figure in his own eyes as just the inability to get into the right spirit of things beyond himself. Beams loom for him where we scarcely discern a mote, the most pardonable of finitudes.

Since the name was dropped, a word here on irony—troublesome neighbor of the witty and the comic. There is a sting to it, the less pardonable as we have been led on, unaware we were being laughed at (*sous cape*, as the French say). Socrates the *eiron*, the unassuming one, was a master at putting the seemingly innocent question, at playing the part of the fellow who simply did not know and had therefore to inquire. Led step by step into the bogland of his own ignorance, the "expert"—artist, theologian, rhetorician—would awake with a start to his hopeless position: hemlock the only lasting cure for so much smiling perfidy. In American parlance, "What are you, a wise guy?" rings out a threat of like, though possibly less dire, retribution. In *Sleeping-Car Murder*, a film by Costa-Gavras, Yves Montand plays a detective investigating a Pullman murder. As he goes through the suspect's living quarters, he pauses before the lampshades, covered as they are with sadistic motifs: "C'est sympathique chez vous [cosy nook]," he remarks in a show of bonhomie. This is a case of indignation phrased in the tones of appreciation, a blow hard to parry without giving yourself away. The violence of irony is muffled, it proceeds by tortuous indirection—reversal, in fact, letting the context force out the straight (that is, contrary) meaning. Not much more than a wry smile is to be expected at best. Hostility diluted, finitude nailed to the post.

In her invaluable social and literary history of the Fool, Enid Welsford (293–94) cites the following passage from N. M. Bernardin's *La comédie italienne en France et les théâtres de la foire et du boulevard, 1570–1791,* which I translate:

> Dominique transformed Harlequin morally . . . turned the greedy clod into a master scoundrel who escapes being hateful by the very exaggeration of his vices, as he leaves the realm of the possible to make his way into unreality, taking us along into the land of pure fancy. Yet as Italian comedy still required an ignorant fool of a servant, the former Harlequin, abandoned by Dominique, doffed his black mask and dipped his face in flour as Pierrot.

The metamorphosis of Harlequin from mocked to mocking fool at the hands of a masterly interpreter, Domenico

Biancolelli (ca. 1670), ensured that the best-known, most long-lived, most versatile figure of the motley fool on the European stage and in the European imagination took on the acrobatic look of the ever-resourceful plotter, giving mind the edge over stomach in the depiction of human folly. Nimble, shrewd, unscrupulous, he embodies the demonic energies to which his name (Hellequin?) makes him heir. His motley suit of vivid patches, a motif for the brush of early Picasso (not unrelated, perhaps, to the cubism still to come), emblematizes the barely contained chaos of primal forces he puts to the service of his young master's amours. There lives in him something of the vigor Plato ascribed to the eight-limbed androgynes of his comic myth, fit to shake up the Olympians on their thrones. His is the active comic role of finitude inflicted.

The figure of pale Pierrot, on the other hand, bathed in melancholy as early as Watteau, rose to heights of augmented pathos throughout the nineteenth century, culminating in Baudelaire's *Vieux saltimbanque* (The Old Acrobat), Kafka's *Hunger Artist,* and Jean-Louis Barrault's unforgettable portrayal of the waiflike Baptiste in the film *Children of Paradise.* Before ever it acquired this self-pitying radiance (as the artist's vision of his broken-down self), it supplied a need equally insistent, filling in the void left by Harlequin's transformation. There is a folly of want of wit as well as one of overly meddlesome wit. Harlequin induces chaos, Pierrot allows it to happen. The couple formed in *Twelfth Night* by Sir Toby Belch and Sir Andrew Aguecheek gives a fair representation of the contrast, the one all hearty mischief making, the other an endearingly fey halfwit; witness this exchange when Andrew comes upon Toby's confederate, Maria:

TOBY: Accost, Sir Andrew.
ANDREW: What's that?

TOBY: My niece's chambermaid.
ANDREW: Good Mistress Accost, I desire better acquaintance.
MARIA: My name is Mary, Sir.
ANDREW: Good Miss Mary Accost.
TOBY: You mistake, knight. "Accost" is front her, board her, woo her, assail her.
ANDREW: By my troth, I would not undertake her in this company. Is that the meaning of "accost"?

Mild befuddlement blends with a commendable eagerness to be instructed, an awestruck wonder before the mysteries of language, to complement his fellow-drinker's verbal exuberance. Quizzed as to his competence as a dancer, he unblushingly admits: "I think I have the back-trick simply as strong as any man in Illyria."

TOBY: Wherefore are these things hid? Wherefore have these gifts a curtain before 'em? Are they like to take dust . . . ? Why dost thou not go to church in a galliard and come home in a corante? My very walk should be a jig. I would not so much as make water but in a sink-a-pace. What dost thou mean? Is it a world to hide virtues in? I did think, by the excellent constitution of thy leg, it was formed under the star of a galliard. (I.iii)

Is it a world to hide virtues in indeed. Sir Toby's is a large affirmative, sufficient to shelter under its shade a round dozen retiring Aguecheeks.

If we cast about for likely successors to this clown pair, upbeat Didi and plaintive Gogo furnish a much watered-down version, Pozzo the autocrat and Lucky the beast of burden, a sadly distorted one, in *Waiting for Godot*. Better to look upon the vacationing Monsieur Hulot as the heir to Pierrot's ineffectual good-will, as he cheerfully sows disaster in his wake, while armed with the best of intentions and the most disconcerting of tennis serves. Uncoordinated innocent that he is, he wanders nonplussed through an uncomprehending world gone to the dogs of modernity, testifying to a lostness we all ought to feel.

Hulot, that Sir Galahad whose trousers do not quite reach the top of his boots, is the last of the romantics. The firm alliance of romance with comedy, from the days of Menander and the shift to so-called New Comedy in the Athens of the fourth century B.C., is a fixture of the comic landscape worth a moment's reflection.

Old Comedy had been a horse of quite another color. Its origins are shrouded in the mists that envelop all beginnings. Aristotle offers the helpful clue that it started as a village revel, a komos, the laughlingly vituperative progress of a band of merrymakers engaging in slanging matches with the bystanders on their way. The song-and-dance routine of the chorus in an Aristophanes play captures this feisty exuberance, disclaiming all semblance of naturalism. Dressed up variously as clouds, as birds, as wasps, as frogs, the chorus establishes a mood of high fantasy in which the zaniest expeditions can be mounted: ascending Olympus on a dung beetle to recapture Peace, founding a new religion on meteorology, calling a sex strike to end a war. A cantankerous old man is generally the hero, one well past his sexual prime, and neither sex nor romance is very much on his mind. There are more pressing issues: war, I.O.U.'s, a plethora of lawsuits. He may plan the founding of a city high up in the clouds, to get away from it all as by the same token he starves the gods into submission by cutting off their supply of sacrificial fumes. Improbability laughingly overcome is the hallmark of Old Comedy, in a spirit akin to that of an undergraduate spoof of their elders. But the freedom of it is as wild as the enigmatic god of the vine, Dionysus—mild and fierce by turns, wreathed in vine leaves, guarded by maenads—could require for the celebration of his festival. Lampooning the powerful, taking violent issue over policies that touched on the survival of the city, comedy exercised to the full the political and religious liberty that could exist in a state where all male citizens ruled and all were present at the play that celebrated the renewal of life under a god of inebriation.

After such hardy fare, invigoratingly free but cut short by military disaster, what New Comedy had to offer may seem tame indeed, but altogether in line with the requirements of existence in a world no longer political, that is, no longer free. Sedate, domestic, plausible, and mostly decorous in the versions that derive from it, in the Roman plays of Plautus and Terence in which this art survives we meet young men in love with slave girls unsuitable as brides, proven freeborn in the end by way of a remembered shipwreck; fathers who watch anxiously over such goings on, forgetful of their own younger days; bustling slaves sent off on a wild goose chase, or devilishly helpful; courtesans who highmindedly and providentially untie the imbroglio. We find ourselves arrayed on the side of impecunious youth, rooting for the underdog, aided and abetted by that under-underdog, the slave. One day, a millennium apart, we will likewise cheer on Molière's disempowered young woman, whose happiness is in the hands of an insanely deluded father, with only the common sense of a chambermaid on her side. Victory in the end, and more especially defeat narrowly averted, powerfully energize the spectator, who cannot help but take sides quite unambiguously with the generally wholesome aspirations of misunderstood, undervalued youth. Laughter is unproblematic when such an ambiance is rendered secure by the firm expectation, embedded in the laws of the genre, that all will be well, for all will end well. Our momentary trepidation is overshadowed by the knowledge that it shall be laid to rest. The perdurability of an alliance that was still holding its own the last time (at this writing) I saw a comedy at the movies, *Roxanne*,[2] may have no more solid basis. We laugh the easier as we are but mildly threatened. The Old Comedy was harsher medicine for tougher stomachs; the New Comedy's durability engenders darker thoughts about the hardihood of the race—or would, were it not that Rabelais, the *Quixote, Ubu, Dr. Strangelove,* and Monty Python's *Meaning of Life* remind us that the Old somehow managed to revive and endure in a variety of formats (one thinks of the George Price cartoons in the *New Yorker*), that all is not lost. It seldom is.

"Love," writes Santayana, "is a red devil at one end of its spectrum, and an ultra-violet angel at the other end" (140). Need we be reminded that the romance of comedy is not as tame as all that, that Tartuffe, who shrinks at the sight of a bosom too much on view, soon palpates Elmire's knee with pious fervor ("Que fait là votre main?" What can your hand be doing there?). This, after Dorine, of the offending décolletage, had already cast in his teeth the mocking observation that "flesh makes quite an impact on your senses," adding for good measure:

> My own desires are not so soon ignited,
> And if I saw you naked as a beast
> Not all your hide would tempt me in the least.
>
> (trans. Wilbur III.ii)

Sex, in other words, rears its ugly head, energizing the bland account I have so far given of the comedy of romance. No word in the language holds a like power of kindling risibility: the very mention of it, the very utterance of the crackling sibilant, *sex*, is enough to start many a jocular expectation. The original comic procession, the

---

[2] In this Hollywood version, Cyrano (nose and all) gets the girl whose love he so richly earned.

komos, was, it is thought, phallic. The ludicrous association of the life force, the majestic principle of universal
renewal, with the tumefaction of those parts of the human
anatomy, male and female, farthest removed from the gaze
of our "higher consciousness," associated moreover with
the excretory function, covered over by what fashion maga-
zines daintily refer to as "intimate apparel," must be looked
upon as a joke of cosmic dimensions.

A fundamental urge mightily put down by one of the
strongest imperatives of social existence, "decency"—the
need, that is, to gain others' respect and to allay their envy,
an urge moreover that can only be satisfied indecorously
(easier, writes Montaigne, to imagine an artisan atop his
wife than a magistrate), an urge finally that stamps with
the seal of pleasure the triumph of the beast in us over the
would-be angel (in Pascal's telling phrase)—surely certifies
us comical. This truth is somewhat wryly acknowledged by
the gentleman who, writing to his son after a review of all
the counsels of reason against the lure of Venus, concludes,
"And besides, my son, the postures are so ridiculous!"

When Sancho discovers that his master's incomparable
Dulcinea is none other than that "sturdy wench" Aldonza
Lorenzo, he cannot restrain his mirth and proceeds to
trumpet forth her manly accomplishments with uproarious
relish. Quixote cuts him short with the following story:

> Once upon a time there was a beautiful widow, young, rich,
> unattached, and, above all, free and easy in her ways, who fell
> in love with a youthful cropped-headed lay brother of large
> and sturdy build. When his superior heard of this, he took
> occasion to speak to the widow one day, giving her a word of
> brotherly reproof. "I am astonished, Madam," he said, "and
> not without a good cause, that a woman of your standing, so
> beautiful and so rich as your Grace is, should be in love with a
> fellow so coarse, so low, so stupid as is So-and-so, in view of
> the fact that there are in this institution so many masters,

graduates, and theologians from whom your Grace might have her pick as from among so many pears, saying, 'This one I like, this one I do not care for.' " She however, answered him with much grace and sprightliness, "You are mistaken, your Reverence, and very old-fashioned in your ideas, if you think that I have made a bad choice by taking So-and-so, stupid as he may appear to be, since so far as what I want him for is concerned, he knows as much and even more philosophy than Aristotle himself." (1:204–5)

The joys of those few lines are many, not least among which the story's issuance from the lips of the chaste hidalgo in justification of his choice of the lady of his undying allegiance. It presents us, first of all, with the simple wish-fulfillment dream of an abbey where the learned masters and austere theologians are openly invited by their superior to compete for the favors of a beautiful young widow of ample means and free-and-easy disposition. That delightful improbability is lent the dignity of a stately, unhurried style of dialogue and narrative that dresses it up in the garments of plausible utterance. But the crux of the risible matter lies in the willed confusion between a conventional and an unconventional sense attributed to learning, the one lodged in the head, the other situated in the loins. The mind's eye is flooded in the end with the highly entertaining tableau of a contest pitting the amatory exertions of the sturdy lay brother against the decidedly feebler performance to be expected in all probability from the prince of philosophers. It all comes down to a feast of interlocking genitalia, humbling to the intellect, glorious for the elated physique with which we side on that occasion.

If we look to the art of Chaplin, of Keaton, of the Marx Brothers for the peculiar twist that projection of the human figure (and much else) on an illuminated screen has brought to the uses of laughter, we find there three distinct variants on the ageless figure of the clown. They hold in common that peculiar attribute of the clown, to be the implausible invariant amid a world that desperately holds on to its own brand of sanity, to business as usual. The world's patent insanity, however (for that is what it is, be it gold rush, civil war, or the singing of an opera), is no match for their zaniness. To begin with, they have the advantage of high recognition value. Invariably, whatever the film's title, its plot, its setting, they appear in their unvarying, highly stylized, and mostly inappropriate getup: the famous oversized shoes and bowler hat, Groucho's painted moustache and cigar, Keaton's whole-body deadpan. They are, moreover, indestructible. Trained acrobats one and all, inured to the demands of the music hall stage, they dispose of their bodies as so many lithe, pliable, projectile properties apt by turns to defy the laws of physics or to make stunning percussive use of them in warding off blows or administering them in return. Objects do their bidding or set upon them perversely, in either case confirming their primary citizenship in the realm of the physical. I know of no better way to convey Keaton's brand of the mastery of motion, here as so often happens in flight, as this sentence from James Agee: "When he ran from a cop his transitions from accelerated walk to easy jogtrot to brisk canter to headlong gallop to flogged-piston sprint—always floating, above this frenzy, the untroubled, untouchable face—were as distinct and as soberly in order as an automatic gearshift" (15). Chaplin, on the other hand, discovered in the opening scene of *City Lights* curled up in the lap of a statue being unveiled to great fanfare, blissfully asleep, demonstrates his uncanny genius for cuddling up to the inhospitable universe and coaxing it to an unwilled bestowal of aid and comfort, or even downright solace. The inhumanity of assembly line work turns into a manic ballet, starvation in the Klondike leads to the sucking of hobnails endowed by his mien with the savoriness of chicken wings. As to Harpo Marx, mute and doll-bewigged in the era of the talkies, he ogles and stalks and honks a message of endearingly futile lechery more expressive than speech. The world's pretensions are made to quail before the uncoordinated assault of that wild trio of zany brothers, just as the world's cruelty finds itself taken on, with ups and downs, by the indomitable Charlie, and its folly pointedly ignored by the super-ingenious Keaton, capable of turning an abandoned ship into a cozy home, or of getting his girl away from a band of cannibals by letting her paddle sitting astride him, supine on the water in his inflated deep-sea diver suit.

Three episodes from their respective film careers sum up the contribution of each to the poetics of laughter.

In *City Lights* the Tramp falls in love with a blind flower girl. The sum of pathos implicit in this donnée (hopeless love, hopeless girl) measures exactly the risk Chaplin is willing to take in comedy. Risk is in fact the very stuff of comedy as he practices the art: the famous scene in which Charlie shows off his rollerskating, backing into but never reaching the edge of an unrailed balcony (of which he is blissfully unaware) is emblematic of that art, which then mocks itself when the skater, made conscious of his peril, loses all composure, quakes ingloriously away from where so recently he sailed. To fall in love, for a clown, is to yield the saving distance that allows him to mock, and defy, and upbraid the world as his role demands, wringing laughter from the folly of those who think themselves wise—an illusion from which his own profession of folly debars him. In his desire to make a difference in the world, the temptation of the world, in fact, is with Chaplin throughout his career as a maker of full-length features—*The Gold Rush, Modern Times, The Great Dictator.* In *Monsieur Verdoux* he will yield up his comic persona; in *Limelight*, falling over the edge, he succumbs to the will to be loved, not for his marvelously inventive brain but for his beautiful soul.

In *City Lights* the peril is held off to, and contained in, the memorable last shot of double recognition, of which Agee writes: "It is enough to shrivel the heart to see, and it is the greatest piece of acting and the highest moment in movies" (10). Before that searing moment, when both are stripped of their illusions, she (now cured of blindness) of her dream of a handsome and rich benefactor, he (fresh out of jail for the "theft" of the money that paid for the cure) of his dream that he could somehow impersonate an acceptable lover—a dream to which he clings for the time of an unbearable look of entreaty—before that perilous moment comedy had more than held its own.

Stripped of all its marvelous farcical side issues (like the effort to subdue the strident hiccups induced by a swallowed whistle), the comedy comes down to a series of deeply mistaken identities. For the blind girl's error let me borrow Walter Kerr's economical description in his splendid *The Silent Clowns:*

> [Charlie] has been mistaken for a millionaire by the blind girl: selling flowers near a busy intersection, she has heard him descend from a limousine, slam its door behind him. Actually, he has simply slipped through it, from one door to the other, to avoid a policeman. But once he has purchased a flower from her—staring in rapture the while—and she hears the door of the departing limousine slam shut again before she can offer proper change she concludes that he is both wealthy and kind. (chap. 36, unpaginated)

Slamming doors both induce and punctuate her error, which only blindness makes possible. Comedy lies deeper than this play of appearances, however beautifully timed. Romance presupposes wealth. Though pure, the girl is not

altogether an innocent. The finer emotions—affection, gratitude—cohabit with our more venal appetites: a poor girl
cannot help wishing. She too then is gently toyed with by
the comedy, brought up sharp against her pardonable limitations (for we pardon ourselves our simple wish-fulfillment
dreams).

Hugged tight in the embrace of a drunken millionaire,
the Tramp endures a more violent transmogrification. Having talked the man out of making an end of himself one
night by drowning in the river, he finds himself drunkenly
promoted friend for life, feted, embraced, partaking in,
recipient of all the considerable largesse at the man's beck
and call. Cold daylight brings a return to a colder reality:
millionaires, like kings, have no friends. "Throw the bum
out" is an order the butler complies with only too gladly.
The seesaw motion is repeated to good effect: nothing too
good for his good friend Charlie amid the night fumes of
drunken revels; sobered up, "out of my sight!" It is the
two-step of comedy, moral equivalent of the saloon swing-
ing door in which Charlie found himself slapped and bat-
tered by turns in an earlier film incarnation. The hoary
figure of the wheel of fortune undergoes a comic acceleration that is reflective both of a larger setting, America's
boom-and-bust economy, and of the wild mood swings of
drunkenness. Charlie, who is all heart, undergoes the ap-
prenticeship of a heartless existence where all fellow feeling
is relegated to the nocturnal blur that alternates with the
bleak, unloving daylight self. The comedy of it, quite aside
from the delirious swing-time pace of it all, lies in the gift
of money pressed on Charlie by night (and for the "theft"
of which the Tramp will be jailed come daylight), blind
fortune's caprice that pays for the cure that restores the
flower girl to sight.

A third moment in this minutely choreographed pas de
trois is that of the clown's own entrapment. The blindness

of the girl, her poverty, her helplessness all conspire to force on Charlie the redemptive mission for which he is only half-suited. As a man, eternally youthful under his ageless appearance, he cannot resist the lure of a chivalric sally on behalf of Beauty oppressed. As a clown he has no business falling in love: his the bracingly recreative, not the procreative, function. His domestication is both prefigured and comically negated in the scene where, in rolling up in a ball the yarn he holds up to her on outstretched hands, she unravels his own raggedy garments, a thread of which got caught up in the yarn. Comedy teeters on the brink of romance, to which it is bound by an age-old compact of mutual aid short of mutual interference. In *City Lights*, at any rate, the spillover is held to a long take in the film's closing moment that conveys no more than a question mark drenched in sentiment.

Gerald Mast puts the transition neatly and pithily: "Whereas Chaplin's films . . . are pointedly social . . . concerned with hunger, humiliation, justice and freedom, Keaton's films seem pointedly pointless" (127). Their fundamental business is to rehearse the "conflict between senseless surrounding and sensible Keaton" (133). Walter Kerr also makes a point of Keaton's stoic at-homeness in a universe to whose laws he quietly and uncomplainingly submits in unpremeditated obedience to the precepts of those Stoic philosophers whose lesson forged the adjective. James Agee, in reproving the comedians of his day for the slackness of their treatment of the visual gag of two who look for each other and fail to meet, gives an account of Keaton's art which cannot be bested and which in spite of its length I therefore quote in full:

> In *The Navigator* Buster Keaton works with practically the same gag. . . . Adrift on a ship which he believes is otherwise empty, he drops a lighted cigarette. A girl finds it. She calls out

and he hears her; each then tries to find the other. First each
walks purposefully down the long, vacant starboard deck, the
girl, then Keaton, turning a corner just in time not to see each
other. Next time around each of them is trotting briskly, very
much in earnest; going at the same pace, they miss each other
just the same. Next time around each of them is going like a
bat out of hell. Again they miss. Then the camera withdraws to
a point of vantage at the stern, leans its chin in its hand and
just watches the whole intricate superstructure of the ship as
the protagonists stroll, steal and scuttle from level to level, up,
down and sidewise, always managing to miss each other by
hair's breadths, in an enchantingly neat and elaborate piece of
timing. There are no subsidiary gags to get laughs in this
sequence and there is little loud laughter; merely a quiet and
steadily increasing kind of delight. When Keaton has got all he
can out of this fine modification of the movie chase he invents
a fine device to bring the two together: the girl, thoroughly
winded, sits down for a breather, indoors, on a plank which
workmen have left across sawhorses. Keaton pauses on an
upper deck, equally winded and puzzled. What follows happens in a couple of seconds at most: air suction whips his silk
topper backward down a ventilator; grabbing frantically for it,
he backs against the lip of the ventilator, jackknifes and falls in
backward. Instantly the camera cuts back to the girl. A topper
falls through the ceiling and lands tidily, right side up, on the
plank beside her. Before she can look more than startled, its
owner follows, head between his knees, crushes the topper,
breaks the plank with the point of his spine and proceeds to
the floor. The breaking of the plank smacks Boy and Girl
together. (19)

Humans in quest of one another are also bodies in motion. The silent screen delineates exquisitely the translation
of intentions into variations of tempo so exactly calibrated
as to let us read the silent minds of the pursued pursuers
as if displayed on a graph. One call sounded would have
brought the mixup to a halt. The silence of the silent era is

thus conscripted into the scenario of delectable error by leaving it quietly out of reckoning. As Agee remarks of him elsewhere in that great essay of his, "Comedy's Silent Era," Keaton "was by his whole style so much the most 'silent' of the silent comedians that even a smile was as deafeningly out of key as a yell" (15). Bergson might have rejoiced in his superlative exploitation of comedy as *du mécanique plaqué sur du vivant*, except that far from a falling off into a mechanistic mode the body Keatonian sails off into heightened grace and velocity, matching the obduracy of an unyielding universe with poltergeist antics of its own that set at naught the laws of physics by yielding to them so absolutely. Body is supreme, mind accommodates to the oily smoothness of its sway.

The Marx Brothers carry into the era of sound the clown's unchallenged mastery of the social space in the silent comedies. They do this by an unprecedented triplication, first of all. They swarm all over the landscape, these three so dissimilar brothers, Groucho careening, Chico more sedate, Harpo sprinting full tilt as satyr to any passing nymph. In addition, they let loose a flow of jabber and honks—Groucho all rudeness and non sequitur, Chico all puns, Harpo all facial mugging—which is to communicative speech as static is to song. That tidewater of non-speech reduces others, moreover, to mostly apoplectic speechlessness. Unlike Buster and Charlie, however, they do not woo in their own person. Theirs is the inheritance of the slaves of Plautus and Terence, Molière's Scapins and Mascarilles: they labor in the service of comely youth (a fourth brother) and make it their business to dispose of unsuitable wooers, obnoxious rivals. Ladies of overripe charms feel the edge of their mockery in equal measure, as it happens: theirs a permanent and a movable (from film to film) charivari.

One scene will do to bring back to mind the flavor of

their antics, the climax of *A Night at the Opera*. No villain more worthily mobilizes their collaborative ire than the self-infatuated bully of an operatic tenor who proposes to make his own the girl of a more worthy tenor's choice. No setting is better suited for the full expression of the trio's anarchic streak, its populist antagonism to the highfalutin', than that symbol of cultural aspirations in America, the opera—preferably headed by a pompous German director, suitably bewhiskered, suitably apoplectic. As they hotfoot it backstage in flight from the inevitable cops, the brothers see for themselves no alternative to shinnying up some convenient backdrop ties out of reach of their pursuers. In unanticipated consequence the fatuous tenor, their enemy, sings his grand aria in Renaissance doublet against a bewildering sliding show of settings ranging from the anachronistic to the bizarre. The diabolical elfins succeed, needless to say, in bringing about the retirement from the scene, in high dudgeon, of the disgraced blowhard—a success that crowns, without the slightest feint at plausibility, a rollicking series of failures. Snatching victory from the jaws of defeat in style is their stock in trade, a victory so palpably implausible as to threaten in no way their standing as the cheerful sowers of comic disaster.

Chico's habit of punning, ranging from the inane to the inspired ("I picked up a little Hungarian (*pause*) and she slapped my face"), invites us to wind down this sampling of the inexhaustible with a look at the pun—that verbal analogue of the proverbial banana peel.

Why do we wince at a pun? Is it perhaps that it is too facile a victory over sense—throwing a switch to derail our train of thought simply by a play of homonym that we were prepared just to take for granted as the "soft underbelly" of communicative speech? a finitude unworthy of remark? A rich congruence can alone redeem a shift downward from the level of sense to the level of sound, too

damagingly ever-available to give unqualified pleasure. The
mind is not so much flooded with unexpected sense as
rudely jolted in its progress toward it. Tripped in fact, as in
the practical joke, which provides amusement on the terms
dictated by malice—the fun being all the other fellow's.
That little Hungarian, on the other hand, slaps our cheek
with all the gusto of a creature born of that invigorating
conjunction: beginner's Magyar and a frisky young maid
that speaks it. A horse—or a filly?—of another color.

Let us end with a joke. The reader may have noted, I
trust with relief, that this survey of the comic has so far
eschewed the telling of jokes that so liberally stud the landscape of most works on the subject. The relative brevity of
the genre lends itself only too readily to the purposes
of illustration. To my mind, it is at the cost of distortion,
given the range and wealth of comic possibilities not so
uniformly foreshortened. In deference, therefore, to the
perverse genius of the comic, this chapter ends on the low
note thus far unindulged, it being laughter's province to
shake up the fastidious.

Two captains[3] were conversing between sea voyages,
and one complained of the nuisance that one of his sailors
was a devilish hand at engaging one and all in wagers that
he invariably won. The other assured him that, thus fore-
warned, he saw no risk in taking the fellow on board for
his next voyage. A few days out to sea, he bemoaned the
pain inflicted by his hemorrhoids, in the sailor's hearing. "I
bet you, captain, fifty dollars that if you retire at night with
a banana up your fundament the pain will be gone in the
morning." What can I lose? the captain said to himself:
either I am cured or I win fifty dollars; and he took on the
wager. The next morning he reported no change and glee-

3 Citation lifted I know not from which of my authors. I beg them all,
in advance, to forgive me, but laughing matter is pretty much common
property (imagine copyrighting a joke).

fully collected on the bet. He could not wait for the voyage to end so he could report that uncommon success to his brother captain. The other struck his brow with a moan: "O my God! He's done it. He bet me five hundred dollars that you were so dumb that he'd get you to stick a banana up your ass before the ship was well under way!"

We were taken in, not a doubt about it, by a circumstance we could not have known. But what we *had* to know, and in our eagerness to follow the thread of the made-up anecdote were willing to forget, is that the odd maneuver forced on the second captain bore a more pungent appellation in the vulgar speech we're all equally familiar with. Mesmerized by the pitfall he knows about, the captain falls into another, that of making a fool of himself. We laugh at both gulls, needlessly aware, hopelessly outmatched, and to the degree that we did not foresee the exact mode of their outwitting we do not mind joining in on our own behalf as well.

CHAPTER EIGHT

Comic Wisdom

Ride si sapis. [Laugh if you be wise.]

—Martial

There is fun in heaven. God can play practical jokes upon Himself, draw chairs away from His own posteriors, set His own turban on fire, steal His own petticoats when He bathes. By sacrificing good taste, this worship achieved what Christianity shirked: the inclusion of merriment.

—*A Passage to India*

Philopaísmones gàr kaì hoi theoí. [For the gods too are fond of a joke.]

—Plato

Is there a way to ascribe to laughter, so closely bound up with folly, a connection with the most prized of our hoped-for attainments, wisdom? Folly, to be sure, when Erasmus slyly rouses her to self-praise in the mock-oration by that title, lays claim to the wisdom of the wise; for is not that wisdom, in the eyes of Paul, folly? and does not a wisdom unsurpassed shine through the folly of the Cross?

Short of such paradoxes, we certainly know of sages who showed a laughing, or at least a smiling, countenance: Thomas More, who needed help ascending the scaffold, reassured the hangman he'd have no trouble coming down again; the Taoist sage Chuang-Tse, seeing his disciples

aghast that he commanded them on his deathbed to leave
his body exposed, inquired why they so favored the ants
over the buzzards. Antiquity readily paired up the tears of
Heraclitus with the laughter of Democritus, and in like
manner Dostoevski counterpointed the grimly ascetic Father Ferrapont with the smilingly accessible, the radiantly
humane, Father Zossima.

Inasmuch as laughter transmutes our frailty to euphoria,
the comic "take" on life bespeaks an undefeated awareness
of even the worst that can befall us. Think of Montaigne
laughingly adducing all the reasons he has not to mind the
kidney stone (it earned him the admiration of all who saw
him bearing up under it; it enlisted him willy-nilly into the
ranks of the Stoics he so much admired from afar; it chas-
tised the part of him where most he sinned). Think of Molière dying practically on stage in the title role of his own
Imaginary Invalid, having mounted the boards while at
death's door to spare his hardworking acting company a
day shorn of earnings. To look one's own death so calmly
in the face bespeaks an acceptance of the inevitable that
surely we may call wisdom.

But perhaps we have so far done no more than argue
the compatibility of wisdom and laughter. What of a more
intimate conjunction of the two concepts? Is there a wisdom that rests squarely on the assumptions of the comic, a
wisdom that is, so to speak, philosophically comic? I believe the following passage from Santayana's "Carnival"
answers the question affirmatively:

> The most profound philosophers . . . deny that any of those
> things exist which we find existing, and maintain that the only
> reality is changeless, infinite, and indistinguishable into parts;
> and I call them the most profound philosophers in spite of this
> obvious folly of theirs, because they are led into it by the force
> of intense reflection, which discloses to them that what exists

is unintelligible and has no reason for existing; and since their
moral and religious prejudices do not allow them to say that to
be irrational and unintelligible is the character proper to existence, they are driven to the alternative of saying that existence
is illusion and that the only reality is something beneath or
above existence. That real existence should be radically comic
never occurs to these solemn sages; they are without one ray
of humour and are persuaded that the universe too must be
without one. (142–43)

Creation itself is in the nature of a cosmic joke, and
this quite independently of the pointlessness so pointedly
caught up in the big bang of our more recent cosmology. A
belief in a divine purpose, however unsearchable, had long
screened from us the knowledge that everything that is
could have been otherwise without its making the least bit
of difference to Anyone. Once that belief evaporated, no
ultimate warrant remained for the existence of a cosmos
or any of its parts, let alone the animated specks on the
surface of an insignificant planet—an atom's worth of mud,
as Voltaire chaffingly called it. To rejoice in the gratuitousness of all-that-is, in the knowledge (or rather the belief)
that it *is* all there is, that the laughter of the All is as
impersonal as it is unaccountable, requires a courage-to-be
of a higher order. It shows a philosophical nerve that it is
only too easy to contrast with the once fashionable angst
before the Nothingness at the heart of Being so recently
still in vogue. Roquentin's discovery of radical contingency
induces the nausea chronicled in Sartre's title. Where comic
wisdom unflinchingly labels the All absurd, the prevailing
winds of philosophy have tended to elevate such cosmic
irresponsibility to the dignity of an infliction, capitalized for
good measure as the Absurd.

Courage, then, is of the essence. It is the strength to
laugh in the face of the abyss that swallowed up our abso-

lutes. First of the cardinal virtues, it is the backbone of our wisdom as well as the premise of our ability to laugh. Small wonder then that we find valor enshrined in that most durable invention of the myth-making imagination in modern times, the laughable tale of the adventures of the Knight of the Mournful Countenance, Don Quixote de La Mancha.

The transition may seem abrupt, from comic wisdom to a rollicking madness, but the close kinship of wisdom and folly is the very theme we are called upon to attend to from the moment we seek to associate wisdom with laughter. Erasmus gave us the clue, in prodding Folly into taking credit for our very being; "for should we have been born," she asks pointedly, "had not our fathers played the fool with our mothers?" Montaigne followed suit as he urged upon us, who are no more than wind, the example of the wind, which does not aspire to anything grander than what lies in its nature—noise and agitation. The counsel of wisdom thus lay for the Bordeaux sage in knowing himself an airy fool.

The hidalgo who fearlessly bestrode the plain of La Mancha in makeshift armor would have none of such advice. He stepped out one day from a book-lined corner of his modest abode, his mind made up to enact on horseback the feats of knight-errantry he had been reading about, to right the wrongs of the world, succor maidens in distress, earn by the strength of his invincible right arm worldwide renown to lay at the feet of the lady of his dreams. Never mind that such a lady did not exist; he invented her on the spot. Never mind that there never *were* knights-errant outside the pages of his romances; it sufficed him to have read about them and then made up his mind to be one. Never mind that he was no doughty warrior but only a wizened, addle-pated old man; he willed himself a hero and rode forthwith in search of adventure.

The joke Cervantes perpetrated on the world by letting loose this unflinching literalist upon an unsuspecting sleepy countryside is so many-faceted that its author himself appeared to have taken stock of it only gradually. Quixote's unshakable belief in the written word, his iron determination to read experience by the map of romance, bending the one to accommodate the other, furnishes occasion for rude buffeting, stoically endured, imperturbably retranslated into the terms of the (to him) relevant literature. The work that has been dubbed the grandfather of the novel establishes the genre on a devastating critique of the novel's trashy antagonist, undiluted romance. To steep yourself in such loose imaginings, it intimates, is to run a serious risk of roaming the countryside on horseback mistaking its landscape of windmills and roadside inns for giants and enchanted castles; for who but a nitwit who does not know the difference could credit the existence of the latter even for the length of a reading?

A serious issue or two lurks beneath the ribbing of one genre by its censorious twin, we recognize. The invincible knight-errant of the romances—today's Indiana Jones, yesterday's Errol Flynn—is a daydream enactment of an incontrovertible need akin to Freud's simple wish fulfillment. The imagination responds supinely to the kneejerk requirements of the psyche: facile reassurance, a ready-made invulnerability, the thrill of Eros on terms of cut-rate heroism. Villains fall by the wayside; grateful maidens shed their bonds to melt into one's arms; victory, though hard-won, is never in serious doubt. Trash, in other words: the opium of the bookworm, that unheroic dreamer of heroic dreams.

The problem is that romance is the novel's flabby twin, that they inhabit the house of fiction on terms of uncomfortable propinquity; hence the animus, the book burning, no less, to which the barber and the curate openly invite us in the sixth chapter of Part One of *The Ingenious Gentleman*

Don Quixote de La Mancha. The indictment of the errant imagination proceeds in the name of a "sane" imagination that is nowhere to be found in the pure state, uncontaminated altogether by the blandishments of romance. Is romance so clearly absent, after all, from such authentically unillusioned novels as *The Red and the Black, Anna Karenina, Portrait of a Lady, The Grapes of Wrath,* to pick a few practically at random? *Don Quixote* may well have launched a genre at odds with itself.

Though such a condition is not without richly comic possibilities—and the string of novella-like entanglements that send a gaggle of star-crossed lovers into the path of unruffled Quixote testify to them within the pages of the *Quixote* itself—the further irony that the hero-as-reader-gone-wrong mistakes literature for life *within the pages of a book* takes the jest to the confines of the metaphysical. The disquisitions of recent literary theorists on the inaccessibility of the referent to what gives itself for such in fiction through the workings of mimesis turn out to have been put to the proof a long time ago in the canvas imagined by Cervantes: a fictional character reaching out for a giant of its own imagining and ending up stuck in the arm of a windmill, itself for all its lance-proof compactness but a squiggle on a page inscribed by the tireless chronicler Cid Hamete Benengeli and patiently deciphered for the reader's benefit by an anonymous narrator. Cervantes delivers to us imperturbably a tale as unlikely as the adventures spun out by his unlikely hero's fevered brain. The "reality" of mill and inn is served up in a book that laughingly rebukes belief.

Yet all this is but learned foreplay to the spectacle provided by the earnestly deluded Quixote charging sheep that he mistakes for an army on the march, windmills he sees as giants flailing their arms at him, winesacks whose blood he sheds at sword's point, while an almost equally deluded Sancho looks on helplessly, the promise of an island growing fainter with every proof of his master's wandering wits. The arresting oddity of the one, extravagantly arrayed in a parody of armor, spouting unearthly challenge at unsuspecting passers-by, is heightened by the contrasting figure of the other, homespun Sancho, who is all low-slung paunch where his master is all bony verticality.

Today we may not laugh so hard as did readers of every age, of every class, of every nation at their first encounter with the pair, before the joke became so embedded in the language, learned in some form from the cradle, as to make *tilting at windmills* as much a shorthand dismissal of a hopeless venture as *quixotic* became a tag to hang on any would-be reformer. To recapture the joke in its freshness we must reread the book, a book too often absorbed by a kind of osmosis out of the bits that found their way into the language or out of unmercifully banalized children's versions. From the first line of a prologue that addresses us as "idling reader" the tone is exquisitely set, for what is the proper reader but an idler, for whose unhurried entertainment, mingling the profit of thoughtfulness with the delight of laughter, that reader-gone-wrong frets himself so untiringly? For does not the latter bestir himself so mightily in the hope of bringing home to the former the worth of the bookish matter with which he himself has fallen hopelessly in love?

Love is the operative word: it holds the key to what elevates the *Quixote* from the rank of superb comic invention to that of a major creation, the comic myth that holds up to us a satisfying representation of human wisdom. It must be remembered that Don Quixote's quest is undertaken under the sign of love. Not only love of the peerless Dulcinea, but the chivalric resolve to loosen the bonds of the oppressed, assure the defense of the weak, beat down the schemes of the villainous. In the grand disquisition on the comparative merits of arms and letters, which concludes in Chapter 38 of Part One, the don eloquently raises the former above the latter insofar as greater hardship is to be endured by the man of arms for the sake of the hard-won blessings of peace and justice. Love of the ease of others enjoins the sacrifice of one's own. Amid the silly prattle of giants and evil necromancers an ideal of genuine care for the welfare of the unwarlike, albeit heavily laced with erotic circumstance—the captive to be freed is more likely than not to be a poignantly comely maiden—quite unmistakably emerges.

That is not to say that love does not enter the equation of the comic. Quite decidedly it does, as attested to by the account earlier quoted (Chapter 7) that the don gives the loudly uproarious Sancho of his willed transfiguration of that lusty peasant lass Aldonza Lorenzo into the incomparable Dulcinea del Toboso ("for what I have need of him Brother So-and-so . . . "). No more delightfully zany episode readily comes to mind, in fact, than that unleashed by a short-lived access of lustiness on the part of the don's blamelessly chaste mount Rocinante in the presence of some mares set to pasture by their Yanguesan masters.

The frisky nag's advances meeting with a cold reception, the Yanguesans intervene on behalf of their mares with a flailing of their long poles, laying the poor beast low. Charged in turn by an indignant Quixote, who sees no harm in enlisting Sancho's half-hearted assistance against the unknightly rabble, they lay into them with a will, flattening master and servant alongside the errant mount. As they lie there, unable to stir hand or foot for the pain in their every bone, Quixote, in answer to Sancho's plaintive query, waxes sententious:

I hold myself to blame for everything. I had no business putting hand to sword against men who had not been dubbed knights and so were not my equals. Because I thus violated the laws of knighthood, the God of battles permitted this punishment to be inflicted upon me. For which reason, Sancho, you should pay attention to what I am about to say to you, for it may have much to do with the safety of both of us. Hereafter, when you see a rabble of this sort committing some offense against us, do not wait for me to draw my sword, for I shall not do so under any circumstances, but rather, draw your own and chastise them to your heart's content. If any knights come to their aid and defense, I will protect you by attacking them with all my might; and you already know by a thousand proofs and experiences the valor of this, my strong right arm. (1:110)

Flat on his back, Quixote prates of invincibility. The hard facts of the case—rustic brawn backed by force of numbers—are swept under the rug of theory. Error alone could have brought him low, human error in the guise of a misreading. The laws of chivalry enjoin upon peace-loving Sancho the duty to draw his sword against any opponent not of noble rank, and they make up the whole number of all such opponents conceivable. Small solace for him in the offer to take on knights nowhere to be met with outside the precincts of his master's imagination. It all sounds so reasonable and it is all so mad; and at the back of our minds there lurks an unworthy thought: is there perhaps not a method in that madness? could the better part of valor, for the one, lie in discretion, leaving the other to take all to himself the hard knocks of their common misadventures? Surely not, but the suspicion adds its spice to the droll mixture.

But though sex does from time to time rear its ugly head upon the stage of Quixote's lofty imaginings—Rocinante's giddiness is premonitory of his master's midnight tussle with the sweaty one-eyed Maritornes, mistaken in the inn where she toils for an uncommonly amorous castellan's daughter—it is love of another sort that prevails in the novel. Master and servant endure so to speak shoulder to shoulder the violence unleashed upon them by their common adherence, however distinct their motives, to a reverie of triumph and vindication steadily rebuffed by an adamantly unheroic yet hardfisted world. Together they seek to reason out their predicament and make sense of the gap between the promise of theory and the bruising setbacks suffered in its application. They approach their authoritative texts each from his own perspective—the one as reader and expounder, the other as unread literalist eager to construe what he hears into the narrowest and most assured of outcomes. One is master and the other servant, to be sure, in a sense so indisputable as to make subordination appear a fact of nature. Yet they enjoy a degree of affectionate equality, nourished by hardship and solitude and sustained by the necessity of constantly reconciling their most divergent points of view on the facts of their common experience, which sets into sharp perspective our well-meaning liberal recoil from the idea of such subordination. The mutuality set in place by a shared delusion translates into an amenity that gradually evolves into mutual affection. There occur between them at times what we might almost look on as lovers' quarrels, as Sancho's rude guffaws sometimes stretch the bounds of permissible hilarity while his master's exalted view of female virtue occasionally erupts into a squall of furious reproof at the servant's unflattering appraisals. They last no longer than such quarrels ever do, against a background of steady comradeship that extends even to their gently companionable mounts, the four of them constituting themselves—the horse, the ass, the knight, and his squire—into the renovated ideal society Northrop Frye postulates for the denouement of all comedy.

All four of them share a like melancholy fate at the end of what we must regard as the most outrageous of Quixote's follies, his forceful liberation of a chain gang of con-

victs bound for the galleys—"unfortunate ones," as he saw
it, "who, much against their will, were being taken where
they did not wish to go" (as the running title of Chapter 22
puts it). Those same unfortunate ones let fly a volley of
stones against their benefactor when he seeks to exact the
ritual pilgrimage to lay their sundered fetters at the lady
Dulcinea's feet:

> They were left alone now—the ass and Rocinante, Sancho and
> Don Quixote: the ass crestfallen and pensive, wagging its ears
> now and then, being under the impression that the hurricane
> of stones that had raged about them was not yet over; Roci-
> nante, stretched alongside his master, for the hack also had
> been felled by a stone; Sancho, naked and fearful of the Holy
> Brotherhood; and Don Quixote, making wry faces at seeing
> himself so mishandled by those to whom he had done so
> much good. (1:177)

What sets this particular adventure apart from all the
others that eventuate, for the most part, in like indignities
visited on the hapless foursome is, in the first place, that
here Quixote acts on his own with no warrant from his
text, for romance nowhere challenges the social order head
on. Furthermore, we readers here for the first time come
close to losing all patience with a brand of folly that endangers our own safety: laughter dies on our lips as, uneasily,
we envisage consequences. To scatter a parcel of malefac-
tors upon the countryside in the name of an ideal of justice
(the courts may have erred) and freedom (they go there
against their will) is a folly that calls upon its own head
swift retribution to be sure, but can we leave it at that?
Others will undoubtedly pay dearly for this particular bit of
illogic, and we only too easily see ourselves in their shoes.
Easy to laugh at a fellow fool enough to charge at a windmill: he'll damage no more than himself, and that at no
more than the cost of a monumental spill. In challenging

the imperfection of human justice, on the other hand, Quixote locates finitude where it continues to hurt us all. No form of chastisement, however harsh, no abrogation of freedom has been devised to this day that does more than curtail the fixed proportion of the human race given to criminality. Quixote's beau geste touches a nerve: the folly of his "solution" mirrors the larger folly of our absence of solution: the laugh is on us.

The challenge to laugh at ourselves may well be the utmost in wisdom that the comic does offer, and the encounter of Quixote with the ruffians who so resolutely turn their backs on his vision of a humanity safe from every kind of oppression (including the yoke of the law) marks a low point in the willingness to laugh thus sympathetically that sets the stage for a remarkable countermovement. The disdain evidenced by Ginés de Passamonte and his minions for what they rightly saw as Quixote's want of the most elementary sense of causation in human affairs is more than matched by the plan set afoot at this point by the curate and the barber of his village to return him to the security of his own roof. It will be remembered that they dress up the fair Dorotea, the first of a quantity of distraught maidens dotting the landscape of the later chapters of Part One, as a bereaved Princess Micomicoma, who swears the valorous knight to the completion of a single adventure: returning her to the throne of which she has been dispossessed by a wicked giant. At the head of a veritable procession of happily reunited swains and maidens issued from a cascade of novellas that all conclude in a major key, Quixote rides home in a cage provided by a magician anxious to deter him from further trouble seeking. It is, we must admit, a rueful kind of embrace of a much diminished heroic folly, but an embrace nevertheless and one that enlists the energies of all the inhabitants of these pages into taking part in a dream they disbelieve in. All, that is, but the one Sancho, open-eyed Sancho who never

mistook an inn for a castle, a windmill for a giant, mischief makers for enchanters, or the flesh-and-blood Dorotea
mooning in corners with her recovered Don Fernando for
the sorrowful Queen of Micomicon. Sancho it is who in the
end proves Quixote's faithful and only true believer, the
sharer of a dream of supernatural valor and of supernatural
doings which alone can sustain his own equally improbable
dream of the governorship of an island.

Sancho is alone perhaps, but in the sequel furnished by
Part Two lonely no longer, for a veritable throng of true
believers have emerged in the only way possible for belief
to arise in these bookish times: from the pages of a book.
We the readers of Part One have been won over to the
existence of Don Quixote de La Mancha and his faithful
squire Sancho Panza: for who has not heard of Quixote and
Sancho, and who cannot cite one or another or perhaps all
their adventures? Their folie à deux is now shared property, we hug it to our bosom, we read the world by its light,
we—in the person of the duke and the duchess, or of the
bachelor Sansón Carrasco—even seek to play a considerable part in it, thereby vulgarizing myth as we literalize
it. For all the heartless pranks they endure in the name
of light ducal entertainment, Quixote blindfolded astride
the flying wooden horse Clavileño, Sancho Solomonic in
the seat of judgment of his long-promised island where the
duke's men seek to play him for the fool he is no longer,
the master and the servant rise to surprising heights of
stoic and unaffected dignity, quietly giving the lie to a
world that prizes its wisdom more highly than their folly.
No reassuring deathbed repentance can outweigh the lighthearted negation of all the world holds dear—its ease,
its possessions, its leaden assurance that the literal is the
true—whereby Quixote seduces first Sancho then every last
one of us duly enchanted readers from the dull acceptance
of what is to the larger freedom of the imagination.

Laughter at a beloved pair who manage to embody between them our heroic aspirations and our more timorous, our more mundane preoccupations partakes of the still unshaken confidence in the human enterprise we associate with the Renaissance. We laugh at a dream of purity, of nobility, of ultimately disinterested fellowship that we yet cannot quite bring ourselves to disavow. Our laughter is still tinged with hope, at the half-ludicrous display of faith and charity made by the superannuated knight and his unlikely squire. Comic wisdom dressed up in such outlandish garb may fail of conviction with an audience brought up on more hard-edged fare. Redolent of the dawn of modern times, *The Ingenious Gentleman Don Quixote de La Mancha* may not make the case for comic wisdom in a manner wholly receivable in an era that looks at modernity itself as a thing of the past, as it rings the death knell of both the individualism and the humanism with which the work of Cervantes is bound up.

In Quixote our finitude steps in as a delusion of grandeur so richly taken to heart as to transcend folly and take on a grandeur of its own. The wisdom that accrues to both Quixote and Sancho through meditation on the genuine pain endured in an imaginary cause enlarges the reader's (the laugher's) understanding of her own condition. Finitude, though properly and joyously apprehended as such, appears in the end enhanced.

What better antidote to a positivity so out of kilter with our contemporary taste for the diminished and the unhinged than that harbinger of post-modernity, Samuel Beckett's *Waiting for Godot, a Tragicomedy in Two Acts*? If we are to laugh, in a key appropriate to the times, at a representation of the human condition that approximates our sense of where on this ravaged and polluted planet we stand, how fitting that we should do so at the spectacle of a pair of derelicts standing about near a ditch in ever-deferred expectation of a meeting with a personage whose

name is a cross of the English word God and the French for
Charlie, Charlot.

Again two men of contrasting character form an apparently ill-assorted but ultimately complementary pair standing resignedly shoulder to shoulder under the buffets of an
unkind fate, wearing the face of weary homelessness together with all the trappings of an end-of-the-road existence. Vladimir and Estragon—the one filled with restless
speculation, as if his Russian surname implied a Slavic
soul, the other stubbornly, whiningly literal-minded, as if
to justify the down-to-earth character of an herb (tarragon)
that gives him his name in French—chase one another in
endless logical circles, passing the empty time of their fruit-
less wait in a running dispute over the way to spend that
time, a dispute that for all its occasional tartness is but the
contentious surface of an ineradicable solidarity. In that pair
stands preserved something of the commonality that arose
so unexpectedly between master and servant in the case of
Quixote and Sancho. The case stands considerably altered
with the latter-day pair, however. Instead of riding to a
firmly held-to delusionary destination, they stay out the
ever-repeated verification of a forever-broken promise.
Rough adversity has made way for destitution and misery,
while grand hopes have been converted into hopelessness just barely held at bay by the width of a slender possibility—the unlikely arrival of that faceless, elusive Godot.

The feminine is absent altogether from the bleak landscape; not so much as a Dulcinea on the horizon, made up
as she was by an act of will. Humanity is here reduced to
the sterile condition implied by its long-adopted single-
gendered appellation, man. The dissociative character of
this representation is brought home more forcefully still by
the appearance in mid-act, repeated in each of the two acts,
of a second pair, the team of Pozzo and Lucky. They seem
to be called upon to enact in its pure state the relation of

subordination which, in the case of Quixote and Sancho, richly conjoined with that of amity and companionship which is here the preserve of the quarrelsome but comradely Gogo and Didi. Pozzo is a kind of circus lion tamer, complacent and heartless, whose beast of burden, staggering at the end of a long rope, is the white-haired bowlerhatted Lucky (what's in a name?). Pointing as they do to the four corners of the European map, the four names lend an air of cosmopolitan generality to the no-man's-land of a barren stage, with its token tree doing service as nature, its ditch speaking to us of the works of man. The two pairs of actors, moreover, meet in mid-act in a kind of cruciform arrangement, the verticality of the power relationship intersected by the horizontality of a pair of equals, overawed by the master, freer than the slave. The arresting spectacle of the preening Pozzo calling on the overburdened Lucky to spare him the slightest exertion comes as the sole dramatic diversion to the purely circular palavers of Gogo and Didi, creating an illusion of drama amid the false starts and blocked moves with which the bickering down-and-outers dissemble their fecklessness.

The cross is by no means out of place in this antimiracle play about waiting for a miracle never to take place—a play that rubs it in, in fact, that salvation is a farcically incongruous outcome to want to tack on to the human adventure. The cross itself is paraded before us in the conundrum Didi extracts from the presence of two thieves crucified on either side of it, in a kind of grandiose preenactment of his and his bedraggled companion's own position.

> VLADIMIR: One of the thieves was saved. (*Pause.*) It's a
> reasonable percentage. (*Pause.*) Gogo.
> ESTRAGON: What?
> VLADIMIR: Suppose we repented.
> ESTRAGON: Repented what?

VLADIMIR: Oh . . . (*He reflects.*) We wouldn't have to go into the details.

ESTRAGON: Our being born?

Vladimir breaks into a hearty laugh which he immediately stifles, his hand pressed to his pubis, his face contorted.

VLADIMIR: One daren't even laugh anymore.

ESTRAGON: Dreadful privation.

VLADIMIR: Merely smile. (*He smiles suddenly from ear to ear, keeps smiling, ceases as suddenly.*) It's not the same thing. (8)

The scriptural reference is as unmistakable as its fall is abrupt into the tomfoolery of shoes and hats. A French audience would be clued in at once by the slightly archaic *larron* in place of the common term for thief, *voleur*. A syllogism is no sooner set going—the thief was saved, let us (likewise) repent—than it is checked in mid-flight. "Repent what?" counters Estragon devastatingly, blotting out by a single interrogative the whole doctrine of the Fall. Vladimir feints with apparent good nature, willing to settle for offhandedness. Estragon shifts from eiron to provocateur, from one who knows not what to repent to one who knows only too well that repentance ties in with a worldview that makes it a sin to have been born. Good-natured full-throated laughter (*un bon rire*) does not often ring on this stage. It is evoked by the cosmic joke of a being consigned to waywardness and error from the cradle. Its expansiveness dies on the lips with a cramp of pubic pain, venereal without a doubt. Sex, in these spent frames, is no more than a residual pain. Laughter diminishes to a grin, smeared on wide, wiped off in the backswing of a two-time beat. Hilarity mocks itself to extinction, just as it had snuffed out high seriousness, or at least hopelessly fractured the discourse on Original Sin, of which the play offers a snuffling, shuffling broken-down reconstruction.

Undeterred, Vladimir goes on worrying the bone of his theological doubts:

VLADIMIR: Where was I . . . How's your foot?
ESTRAGON: Swelling visibly.
VLADIMIR: Ah yes, the two thieves. Do you remember the
story?
ESTRAGON: No.
VLADIMIR: Shall I tell it to you?
ESTRAGON: No.
VLADIMIR: It'll pass the time. (*Pause.*) Two thieves, crucified at
the same time as our Saviour. One—
ESTRAGON: Our what?
VLADIMIR: Our Saviour. Two thieves. One is supposed to have
been saved and the other . . . (*He searches for the contrary of
saved*) . . . damned.
ESTRAGON: Saved from what?

Once again Gogo devastates. Salvation is stopped in its
tracks by its homely twin meaning, which alone finds passage to his willfully uneducated ear. Clinging to the lowly
realities of ditch and shoes and nightly beatings, he admits
of no meaning grander to the word *save* than that of rescue. Vladimir, if only to pass the time, stumbles on:

VLADIMIR: And yet . . . (*pause*) . . . how is it—this is not
boring you I hope—how is it that of the four Evangelists
only one speaks of a thief being saved. The four of them
were there—or thereabouts—and only one speaks of a thief
being saved. (*Pause.*) Come on, Gogo, return the ball, can't
you, once in a way?
ESTRAGON: (*with exaggerated enthusiasm*) I find this really most
extraordinarily interesting.
VLADIMIR: One out of four. Of the three two don't mention
any thieves at all and a third says that both of them abused
him.
. . . .
ESTRAGON: Well what of it?
VLADIMIR: Then the two of them must have been damned.
ESTRAGON: And why not?

VLADIMIR: But one of the four says that one of the two was
saved.
ESTRAGON: Well? They don't agree and that's all there is to it.
VLADIMIR: But all four were there. And only one speaks of a
thief being saved. Why believe him rather than the others?
ESTRAGON: Who believes him?
VLADIMIR: Everybody. It's the only version they know.
ESTRAGON: People are bloody ignorant apes. (9)

The French "Les gens sont des cons" (People are assholes)
is far more brutally dismissive of the whole matter. Estragon's intolerance is bracing, Vladimir's persistence en-
dearing, as he tosses his figures about with laudable care
for a truth that recedes further and further into confusion.
The issue is, after all, momentous: Faith with a capital letter
hangs on the faith, the credence that can be accorded the
consecrated witnesses of the central drama of the Crucifixion. An odd mix of omission and contradiction renders the
case, in the phrase now so much in fashion, undecidable.
On such shaky grounds theology invites the public to stake
their hopes. Estragon's uncompromising highhandedness
practices a reduction of the whole matter that not only
throws it out of court but throws out the court as well (les
gens sont . . .). Four gospels hopelessly at odds, the matter
broached with the oddest inappropriateness ("It'll pass the
time"; "return the ball"), a verdict passed on it as emphatic
as that of the Queen of Hearts, make for a comic mixture
as difficult to define as I at least find it hard to resist.

Quixote's faith in his balmy authorities pitting knighthood against necromancy was absolute. Vladimir's perplex-
ities, Estragon's dismissiveness are aimed at the Gospel,
the text of which all others within the ambit of the West
merely adumbrate the authority. Authority itself has nowa-
days come into question, and our bowler-hatted clowns,
butting into one another in a manner inherited from a mil-

lenary circus tradition, "pass the time" getting nowhere as the fully certified representatives of our lostness. Nothing so solid as a windmill left on the horizon to beckon us to a charge.

Theology has its day at the hands of Didi and Gogo, the one all earnest puzzlement, the other all shrewdly obtuse recalcitrance. The political order will have its turn in the grim pair at either end of a long rope: Pozzo, overbearing and self-infatuated; Lucky, brutishly subservient. The representation of unmitigated oppression holds little promise of irresistible comicality, and we may well wonder how it can be rendered simply bearable. A look at stage directions that practically eat up all the textural space on the page that discloses their first appearance brings it all back to mind:

> *Enter Pozzo and Lucky. Pozzo drives Lucky by means of a rope passed round his neck, so that Lucky is the first to enter, followed by the rope which is long enough to let him reach the middle of the stage before Pozzo appears. Lucky carries a heavy bag, a folding stool, a picnic basket and a great coat, Pozzo a whip.* (15)

All loud complacency, Pozzo treats his bemused audience to some lordly chit-chat, waited on all the while by the mutely attentive Lucky hand and foot:

> POZZO: . . . Up pig! (*Pause.*) Every time he drops he falls asleep. (*Jerks the rope.*) Up hog! (*Noise of Lucky getting up and picking up his baggage. Pozzo jerks the rope.*) Back! (*Enter Lucky backwards.*) Stop! (*Lucky stops.*) Turn! (*Lucky turns. To Vladimir and Estragon, affably.*) Gentlemen, I am happy to have met you. (*Before their incredulous expression.*) Yes yes, sincerely happy. (*He jerks the rope.*) Closer! (*Lucky advances.*) Stop! (*Lucky stops.*) . . . (*To Lucky.*) Coat! (*Lucky puts down the bag, advances, gives the coat, goes back to his place, takes up the bag.*) Hold that! (*Pozzo holds out the whip. Lucky advances and, both his hands being occupied, takes the whip in his mouth, then goes*

*back to his place. Pozzo begins to put on his coat, stops.) Coat!
(Lucky puts down bag, basket and stool, advances, helps Pozzo on
with his coat, goes back to his place and takes up bag, basket and
stool.)* Touch of autumn in the air this evening. (16)

No more ferociously economical portrayal of the social
order could be devised than this counterpoint of the blith-
eringly banal and the unblushingly tyrannical. The ballet of
unreasonable demand met by insanely punctilious exertion
so neatly captures injustice as to remove its sting. We laugh
ruefully, as we do at all caricature, for hitting on the nose
the sum of our least forgivable failings.

Pity does not mar our grim amusement. Lucky is as
unapproachable as he is downtrodden. He weeps when he
learns that his master is taking him to market to sell him,
but Gogo earns himself a swift kick in the shins for coming
near him handkerchief in hand. Invited to think for the
entertainment of the company, Lucky, once his hat is refas-
tened on his snowy locks (sixty years now has he been in
Pozzo's service), opens up in the funereal manner of a
broken record:

LUCKY: Given the existence as uttered forth in the public
works of Puncher and Wattmann of a personal God
quaquaquaqua with white beard quaquaquaqua outside time
without extension who from the heights of divine apathia
divine athambia divine aphasia loves us dearly with some
exceptions for reasons unknown but time will tell . . . but
not so fast and considering what is more that as a result of
the labors left unfinished crowned by the Acacacacademy of
Anthropopopometry of Essy-in-Possy of Testew and Cunard
it is established beyond all doubt all other doubt that that
which clings to the labors of men that as a result of the
labors unfinished of Testew and Cunard it is established as
hereinafter but not so fast . . . (28)

The stentorian flood of near-nonsense dressed up in gar-
bled academic phraseology cannot be turned off until in
exasperation the three of them tackle Lucky and tear off his
hat in a flurry of legitimate self-defense. So much for vox
populi. Master and slave move on, the boy bearing regrets
from Mr. Godot appears, night falls abruptly to end Act
One.

Act Two is consumed in part in denial on Estragon's part
that Act One ever occurred. Vladimir patiently recon-
structs: Lucky gave him a kick, Pozzo handed out some
bones after his meal, they had considered hanging themselves from that tree. Don't you recognize it? "Recognize!"
Gogo explodes, "What is there to recognize? All my lousy
life I've crawled about in the mud! And you talk to me
about scenery!" (39). They're off and running. Nothing is
changed, it is yet another day of filling in time as they
wait for Godot. Didi still thinks up conversational gambits,
Gogo still digs in his heels. The return of Lucky and Pozzo
imports drama once more into the antidrama of a dialogue
programmed to go nowhere. The world of insane command and abject obedience, the "real world," is where
change occurs, where novelty is possible. Pozzo is now
blind. Lucky stops at the sight of the derelicts. Pozzo
comes crashing into him, they both sprawl. Gogo and Didi
give earnest consideration to Pozzo's piteous cries to be
helped up. Theirs the upper hand now: whereas the day
before they stood in awe of the imperious, the lordly
Pozzo, they now philosophize at leisure on the opportune-
ness of giving him a hand. After some rough treatment to
shut him up they relent at last. The change, they discover,
is more apparent than real. Pozzo is now helpless, but
Lucky is still his slave. As they get under way, Didi asks
about the contents of the bag Lucky totes. Sand, he learns.
Off the pair stumbles, and they are heard to crash offstage.
Hegel's master-slave dialectic has pretty well been liter-

alized—but for all that, master still has hold of the right end of the rope, slave still toils on under a load of sand. This time Lucky has not been heard to think on command or to sing. Sing?

POZZO: But he is dumb.
VLADIMIR: Dumb!
POZZO: Dumb. He can't even groan.
VLADIMIR: Dumb! Since when?
POZZO: (*suddenly furious*). Have you not done tormenting me with your accursed time! It's abominable! When! When! One day, is that not enough for you, one day he went dumb, one day I went blind, one day we'll go deaf, one day we were born, one day we shall die, the same day, the same second, it that not enough for you? (57)

Irate sententiousness meets one's mildest queries, here as in *Alice in Wonderland*. Pozzo's exit speech, harbinger of the second nightfall, the second message of easily disbelievable regrets and promise that will close the play in perfect stasis—

VLADIMIR: Well? Shall we go?
ESTRAGON: Yes, let's go.
They do not move.

—sums up the joke of mortality we are invited to take in, if not laughingly at any rate knowingly. To be human is not much: Pascal likened us to a reed—adding, by way of solace, a thinking reed. Acerbic Beckett dresses up our littleness in the rags of destitution, inviting us to wait out the ever-deferred punch line of the cosmic joke in whatever paltry comfort we can wryly fashion for ourselves.

Not unlike the systole and diastole of the heart valves, the chest expanding in aspiration only to contract in expiration, the road to enchantment traveled by Quixote trails into the bleak, the narrow stage of disenchantment on which Didi and Gogo stand marooned. The laughter that greeted the earlier pair was at first incredulous before such a parcel of willful blindness intermixed with grandiloquent delusion. As, gradually, we took in the rich complexion of an error that consisted of taking the world for a fairer and a stranger place than it is, we ended up wishing it worthy of Quixote's highminded, Sancho's guileless, quest. The chastened laughter with which we greet the mirthless antics of our latter-day seekers after cold comfort partakes of a rueful sense that they speak for the stripped-down spiritual condition we inhabit, where hope peeps out of a chink that merely opens up on hopelessness held at bay—for just another day.

Is it wisdom, then, thus to laugh out of both sides of our mouth, so to speak: at those, that is, who cannot be made to see life for what it is, and also at those who think they see it only too well? It may well be that in that gaping interval a laughing apprehension of the human condition has its legitimate scope. The thoughtful laughter that salutes finitude wryly where it touches all that we are and that we hope (or fear) to be, whether defiantly heroic or disabusedly antiheroic, is laughter writ large. In the one case we laugh at ourselves, inasmuch as we are mad enough to take on the world on our own terms entirely. In the other we laugh at the world for being so palpably a place of senselessness and absurdity, a cruel enigma whose solution is from day to day deferred. A sunny wisdom invites us to make little of ourselves; a wintry wisdom bids us recognize the little we can expect from the world. Courage, the courage Santayana preached by laughing example, shines through either comic paradigm. Quixote's entirely misplaced valor dims to unillusioned endurance of lowlife grit in his homeless, derelict successors. We are not called upon to pity ourselves through the example of either, for both are ornery enough to oblige us to keep our distance. The courage to laugh at a case so close to our own—the delusionary folly that a world is out there for us to mend, the bleak recognition that we wait in vain for Someone to mend *us*—is vouchsafed us by that saving distance.

In the end let it be said: to laugh in the face of folly (our own) and lostness (our own), however wistfully, is to reach for the prize of wisdom, inglorious perhaps, unlikely to win us the crown of a saint or mantle of a guru but secure in the unfazed recognition of the little we are—so much wind, as Montaigne reminds us, but for all that content to make a noise in the world, glad simply to be.

Conclusion

In the balance of existence pain may or may not outweigh pleasure; there is no way to decide. The assessment
is a matter of both temperament and personal experience,
both immensely variable, neither authoritative or gener-
alizable. The Greeks—for one must always turn back to the
Greeks for apposite reflection on questions of human import—devised the twin spectacle of tragedy and comedy to
accommodate the one and the other and recognize their
nearly equal claim on our earthly span. The one enactment
accords pity and terror their due, in recognition of the more
awesome side of human experience where the mightiest are
brought low in a devastating manner wholly out of proportion with the error of their ways. The other gives us to
understand how we bumble and fail, how ill-bestowed is
our self-regard, how little it takes to send us sprawling, all
to the hoots and cackles of an audience seated at a safe
remove from the spectacle of their own littleness, which is
exposed to no drastic comeuppance, no irremediable fate.
The shadow of death that looms over tragedy lifts when it
is comedy's turn, leaving in place the mad buoyancy of life,

an urgency that jostles but does not kill. In tragedy death leaves in place a sense of our worth, the hero dying unbelittled by his fate. Comedy merely knocks us about, sparing of our life at the cost of our dignity.

Mortality is the dread visage of our finitude: easier to laugh off our fear of it than the fact of our coming extinction. The domain of the comic is vast, but it stops at the line we cross into sorrow and loss brought on by our mortal condition. Gravity is enthroned there, pressing on us the urgency of taking our affairs to heart. It is the inaccessibility of what we regard as our deeper feelings to the laughable mode, except by way of parody and transposition, that confines the comic to the nether sphere of the aesthetic domain, to the "un-serious."[1] The joyous awareness of limitedness, however, cannot but find confirmation in its own belittlement. There is no cause for wishing to claim for the comic an unlimited compass: limitation is what it is all about. And when we consider that so emphatically delimited a scope embraces all in life that smacks of the inextinguishable gush of aliveness, its reverses that do not hobble, its blows that do no lasting damage, its endurance, its elasticity, its bounce, we find no reason to mope that laughter does stop somewhere. The point is, it carries us far enough, far enough to live our lives as lightheartedly as it is given us to exercise that invaluable faculty.

Laughter, for all that, is not to be dismissed as of no moment. It is not to be taken at its own low valuation. The view of it propounded in these pages, though it lets it celebrate the victory of something small over something

---

[1] In his "Modest Proposal," Swift exaggerates to good effect the very real savagery of English management of Irish affairs by taking it over the line into cannibalism. To slaughter Irish babes and sell them for meat is to solve at one stroke the problem of famine and that of overpopulation. Very *serious* sorrows are dealt with in a manner that, in the last analysis, is less *un-serious* than the governmental pieties it mocks. The inverted commas are very much in order around that adjective in my text.

great— of pebble over spear, David over Goliath, pin prick over balloon—does not take that celebration as a mark of smallness. In laughter resides the power to tap the unending energies present in the sum of all that defeats us. Finitude is no more or less than the name of that *all*. Wherever we stumble we may laugh, granted the conditions of timing and emotional remove spoken of in the body of this essay. The sum of our failures goes into the creation of a moment of euphoric invulnerability that is unendingly repeatable. That selfsame accrual of strength that flowed into the veins of the giant Antaeus whenever he took a fall on the bosom of his mother Earth humankind has at its own disposal from every miss that is turned into a hit by the touch of a receptive funny bone.

Seen as the easily overlooked instrumentality of such a transmutation, laughter emerges as the wild card in the pack of our faculties, the one to which we owe the capacity to negotiate our perilous freedom. Earlier views have taught us a sense of its anarchic, its subversive, character. Some have seen in it the embodiment of all that is still unfettered in our nature. Its spontaneity, its power to lift inhibitions, have allied it to childhood play. We seek for it, in our own view of the matter, an even larger dispensation. As the joyous consciousness of our finitude, the capacity to be amused at what holds us in check bespeaks an awesome resilience. It endows human nature with the means to turn the corner, perpetually, on the disasters sown in its path by its own freedom from instinctual programmation. It makes that very freedom possible by rendering it manageable. Standing unobtrusive guard over our right to be wrong, laughter ensures that the animal that is so badly in need of a sense of humor (Mindess) may go on floundering for as long as it does not too catastrophically overstep the boundaries of the safely laughable.

Bibliography

Agee, James. *Agee on Film*. New York: McDowell, Obolensky, 1958.

Ambrose, Anthony. "The Age of Onset of Ambivalence in Early Childhood: Indications from the Study of Laughter." *Journal of Child Psychology and Psychiatry* 4 (1963): 167–81.

Apte, Mahadev. *Humor and Laughter: An Anthropological Approach.* Ithaca: Cornell University Press, 1985.

Apter, M. J., and K. C. P. Smith. "Humour and the Theory of Psychological Reversals." In *It's a Funny Thing*, ed. A. J. Chapman and H. C. Foot, pp. 95–100.

Aristotle. *Parts of Animals*, trans. A. L. Peck. Loeb Classical Library. Cambridge: Harvard University Press, 1968.

———. *Poetics*, trans. S. H. Butcher. New York: Hill and Wang, 1961.

———. *Problems*, trans. W. S. Hett. 2 vols. Loeb Classical Library. Cambridge: Harvard University Press, 1936.

Aubouin, Elie. *Les genres du comique*. Marseilles: O. F. E. P., 1948.

Bacon, Helen. "Socrates Crowned." *Virginia Quarterly* 35 (1959): 415–30.

Bain, Alexander. *The Emotions and the Will*. London, 1859.

Bastide, Georges. "Le rire et sa signification éthique." *Revue Philosophique* 139 (1949): 288–306.

Bataille, Georges. *La somme athéologique* I. Paris: Gallimard, 1973. Vol. 5 of *Oeuvres complètes.* 9 vols. 1970–79.

Bateson, Gregory. "The Position of Humor in Human Communication." In *Cybernetics,* ed. Heinz von Foerster. New York: Josiah Macy, Jr. Foundation, 1953.

Baudelaire, Charles. "De l'essence du rire et généralement du comique dans les arts plastiques." In *Curiosités esthétiques.* Paris: Louis Conard, 1923, pp. 369–96.

Beckett, Samuel. *Waiting for Godot: A Tragicomedy in Two Acts.* New York: Grove Press, 1954.

Berge, Dr. André, et al., eds. *Introduction à l'étude scientifique du rire.* Paris: Flammarion, 1959.

Bergson, Henri. *Laughter* In *Comedy,* ed. W. Sypher. Baltimore: Johns Hopkins University Press, 1956, pp. 61–260.

——. *Le rire, essai sur la signification du comique* [1900]. Paris: Presses Universitaires de France, 1956.

Berlyne, D. E. "Laughter, Humor, and Play." In *Handbook of Social Psychology,* vol. 3, ed. Gardner Lindzey. New York: Random House, 1969, pp. 795–852.

Bernardin, Napoléon Maurice. *La comédie italienne en France et les théâtres de la foire et du boulevard (1570–1791).* Paris: Edition de la Revue bleue, 1902.

Blake, William. "The Marriage of Heaven and Hell." In *Prose and Poetry,* ed. Geoffrey Keynes. London: Nonesuch, 1956, pp. 181–93.

Bossuet, Jacques-Bénigne. *Maximes sur la comédie.* Versailles, 1818. Vol. 37 of *Oeuvres.* 43 vols. 1815–19.

Bradney, Pamela. "The Joking Relationship in Industry." *Human Relations* 10 (1957): 179–87.

Caldwell, J. R. *Studies in the Comic.* Berkeley: University of California Press, 1941.

Castelvetro, Ludovico. *Commentary on Aristotle's "Poetics"* [1577].

Cave, Terence. *The Cornucopian Text: Problems of Writing in the French Renaissance.* Oxford: Clarendon Press, 1979.

Cervantes [Miguel de Cervantes Saavedra]. *Don Quixote,* trans. Samuel Putnam. 2 vols. New York: Viking, 1949.

Chapiro, Marc. *L'illusion comique.* Paris: Presses Universitaires de France, 1940.

Chapman, Antony J. and Hugh C. Foot, eds. *Humour and Laughter: Theory, Research, and Applications.* London: Wiley, 1976.

——. *It's a Funny Thing, Humour: International Conference on Laughter and Humour*. New York: Pergamon, 1977.

Charney, Maurice. *Comedy High and Low: An Introduction to the Experience of Comedy*. New York: Oxford University Press, 1978.

——. "Comic Creativity in Plays, Films, and Jokes." In *Handbook of Humor Research*, ed. P. E. McGhee and J. H. Goldstein 1983, 2:33–40.

——, ed. *Comedy: New Perspectives*. Special issue of *New York Literary Forum* 1 (1978).

Chaucer, Geoffrey. *Canterbury Tales*. Everyman's Library. New York: E. P. Dutton, 1941.

Chesterfield, Philip Dormer Stanhope, 4th earl of. *Letters to His Son*. 3 vols. London, 1810.

Chesterton, G. K. "Humour." *Encyclopaedia Britannica*. 11th ed. Cambridge: Cambridge University Press, 1910.

Cicero, Marcus Tullius. *De Oratore*. 2 vols. Loeb Classical Library. Cambridge: Harvard University Press, 1942.

Coleridge, Samuel T. *The Literary Remains*. 4 vols. London, 1836.

Cooper, Lane. *An Aristotelian Theory of Comedy*. New York: Harcourt, Brace, 1972.

Corneille, Pierre. *Théâtre*, ed. Pierre Lièvre. 2 vols. Bibliothèque de la Pléiade. Paris: Gallimard, 1950.

Corrigan, Robert W. *Comedy: Meaning and Form*. San Francisco: Chandler, 1965.

Cousins, Norman. *Anatomy of an Illness as Perceived by a Patient*. New York: W. W. Norton, 1979.

Davis, Jessica R. Milner. "A Structural Approach to Humour in Farce." In *It's a Funny Thing*, ed. A. J. Chapman and H. C. Foot, pp. 391–94.

Davis, Natalie Zemon. "Women on Top." In *Society and Culture in Early Modern France*. Stanford: Stanford University Press, 1975, pp. 124–51.

Descartes, René. "Les passions de l'âme." *Oeuvres et lettres*, ed. André Bridoux. La Bibliothèque de la Pléiade. Paris: Gallimard, 1953, pp. 795–802.

Diderot, Denis. *Rameau's Nephew*, trans. Jacques Barzun. New York: Random House, 1956.

Dinesen, Isak. *Out of Africa* [1938]. New York: Random House, 1972.

Donatus, Aelius. *Aeli Donati quod fertur commentum in Terenti* [c. 350 C.E.], ed. P. Wessner. 3 vols. Leipzig, 1902.

Douglas, Mary. "Do Dogs Laugh? A Cross-Cultural Approach to Body Symbolism." *Journal of Psychosomatic Research* 15 (1971): 387–90.

Dryden, John. Preface to *An Evening's Love or The Mock Astrologer* [1671]. Berkeley: University of California Press, 1970. Vol. 10 of *The Works of John Dryden*, ed. E. N. Hooker and H. T. Swedenberg, Jr. 20 vols. 1956–84.

Duchowny, Michael S. "Pathological Disorders of Laughter." In *Handbook of Humor Research*, ed. P. E. McGhee and J. H. Goldstein, 1983, 2:89–108.

Dumont, Léon. *Théorie scientifique de la sensibilité.* Paris, 1877.

Dupréel, Ernest. "Le problème sociologique du rire." *Revue Philosophique de la France et de l'Etranger* 106 (1928): 213–60.

Eastman, Max. *Enjoyment of Laughter.* New York: Simon and Schuster, 1929.

Emerson, Ralph Waldo. "The Comic" [1843]. Vol. 8 of *The Complete Works*, ed. J. E. Cabot. Boston: Houghton Mifflin, 1903. 12 vols. 1903–4.

Erasmus, Desiderius. *The Praise of Folly* [1511], trans. H. H. Hudson. Princeton: Princeton University Press, 1941.

Fabre, Lucien. *Le rire et les rieurs.* Paris: Gallimard, 1929.

Fernandez, Ramon. *La vie de Molière.* Paris: Gallimard, 1939.

Ferroni, Giulio. *Il comico nelle teorie contemporanee.* Rome: Bulzoni, 1974.

Fielding, Henry. *Joseph Andrews.* London: Folio Society, 1967.

Fine, Gary Alan. "Humour in Situ: The Role of Humour in Small Group Culture." In *It's a Funny Thing*, ed. A. J. Chapman and H. C. Foot, pp. 315–18.

Fisher, Rhoda, and Seymour Fisher. "Personality and Psychopathology in the Comic." In *Handbook of Humor Research*, ed. P. E. McGhee and J. H. Goldstein, 2:41–59.

———. *Pretend the World Is Funny and Forever.* Hillsdale, N.J.: Erlbaum, 1981.

Forster, E. M. *A Passage to India* [1924]. New York: Harcourt, Brace, 1952.

Fourastié, Jean. *Le rire, suite.* Paris: Denoël-Gonthier, 1983.

Fowler, Henry Watson. *A Dictionary of Modern English Usage.* Oxford: Clarendon Press, 1927.

Freedman, D. G. "Smiling in Blind Infants and the Issue of Innate vs. Acquired." *Journal of Child Psychology and Psychiatry* 5 (1964): 171–84.

Freud, Sigmund. "Civilization and Its Discontents" [1929]. Vol. 21
of the *Standard Edition of the Complete Psychological Works*, trans. J.
Strachey. 64–145. London: Hogarth Press, 1961. 24 vols. 1961–
74.
———. "Humour" [1927]. Vol 21 of the *Standard Edition*. 159–66.
———. *Jokes and Their Relation to the Unconscious* [1905]. Vol. 8 of the
Standard Edition.
———. *Der Witz und seine Beziehung zum Unbewussten*. Leipzig: Franz
Denticke, 1905.
Fry, William F., Jr. "The Appeasement Function of Mirthful
Laughter." In *It's a Funny Thing*, ed. A. J. Chapman and H. C.
Foot, pp. 23–26.
Frye, Northrop. *Anatomy of Criticism*. Princeton: Princeton Univer-
sity Press, 1957.
———. *A Natural Perspective*. New York: Columbia University Press,
1965.
Fussell, B. H. "A Pratfall Can Be a Beautiful Thing." In *Comedy:
New Perspectives*, ed. M. Charney, pp. 243–57.
Giles, Howard, and Geoffrey Oxford. "Towards a Multidimension-
al Theory of Laughter Causation and Its Social Implications."
Bulletin of British Psychological Sociology 23 (1970): 97–105.
Goldstein, Jeffrey H. "Cross-Cultural Research: Humour Here and
There." In *It's a Funny Thing*, ed. A. J. Chapman and H. C.
Foot, pp. 167–74.
Goldstein, Jeffrey, and Paul McGhee, eds. *The Psychology of Humor*.
New York: Pergamon, 1977.
Gombrich, E. H. *Art and Illusion*. New York: Pantheon, 1961.
Grotjahn, Martin. *Beyond Laughter*. New York: McGraw Hill, 1957.
Guillaumin, Jean. "Freud entre les deux topiques: Le comique
après 'L'Humour' (1927), une analyse inachevée." *Revue Fran-
çaise de Psychanalyse* 37 (1973): 607–54.
Gurewitch, Morton. *Comedy: The Irrational Vision*. Ithaca: Cornell
University Press, 1975.
Gutwirth, Marcel. "Réflexions sur le comique." *Revue d'Esthétique*
17, nos. 1–2 (1964): 7–39.
Hall, Stanley, and Arthur Allin. "The Psychology of Tickling and
Laughter." *American Journal of Psychology* 9 (1897): 1–41.
Halperin, David M. *Before Pastoral: Theocritus and the Ancient Tradi-
tion of Bucolic Poetry*. New Haven: Yale University Press, 1983.
Hegel, Georg Wilhelm Friedrich. *Aesthetics*, trans. T. M. Knox. 2
vols. Oxford: Clarendon Press, 1975.

Heller, Joseph. *No Laughing Matter*. New York: Putnam, 1986.
Hinde, Robert A., ed. *Non-Verbal Communication*. Cambridge: Cambridge University Press, 1972.
Hobbes, Thomas. "Human Nature." London, 1840. Vol. 4 of *Works*. 11 vols. 1839–45.
Hooff, J. A. R. A. M. van. "A Comparative Approach to the Philogeny of Laughter and Smiling." In *Non-Verbal Communication*, ed. R. A. Hinde, pp. 209–41.
Horgan, D. "Learning to Tell Jokes: A Case of Metalinguistic Abilities." *Journal of Child Language* 8 (1981): 217–24.
Huizinga, Johan. *Homo Ludens*. Boston: Beacon Press, 1955.
Hyers, M. Conrad, ed. *Holy Laughter: Essays on Religion in the Comic Perspective*. New York: Seabury, 1969.
Ironside, Redvers. "Disorders of Laughter Due to Brain Lesions." *Brain* 79 (1956): 589–609.
Issar, Naresh, S. Y. W. Tsang, L. LaFave, A. Guilmette, and K. Issar. "Ethnic Humour as a Function of Social-Normative Incongruity and Ego-Involvement." In *It's a Funny Thing*, ed. A. J. Chapman and H. C. Foot, pp. 281–82.
Jarry, Alfred. *Ubu roi*, trans. Barbara Wright. New York: New Directions, 1961.
Johnson, Samuel. *The Rambler*, ed. W. J. Bate and A. B. Strauss. 3 vols. New Haven: Yale University Press, 1969.
Jung, Carl G. "On the Psychology of the Trickster Figure." In P. Radin, *The Trickster* pp. 195–211.
Kant, Immanuel. *Kritik der Urteilskraft*. Berlin: G. Riner, 1915. Vol. 5 of *Gesammelte Schriften*. 29 vols. 1910 to date.
Kerényi, Karl. "The Trickster in Relation to Greek Mythology." In P. Radin, *The Trickster*, pp. 173–91.
Kerr, Walter. *The Silent Clowns*. New York: Knopf, 1975.
Koestler, Arthur. *The Act of Creation*. New York: Macmillan, 1964.
——. *Insight and Outlook*. 2 vols. New York: Macmillan, 1949.
Kris, Ernst. "Ego Development and the Comic." *International Journal of Psychoanalysis* 19 (1939): 77–90.
——. "Laughter as an Expressive Process: Contributions to the Psychoanalysis of Expressive Behavior." In *The World of Emotions*, ed. C. Socarides, pp. 87–107.
——. *Psychoanalytic Explorations in Art*. New York: International Universities Press, 1962.
La Fave, Lawrence, J. Haddad, and W. A. Maesen. "Superiority, Enhanced Self-Esteem, and Perceived Incongruity Humour The-

ory." In *Humour and Laughter,* ed. A. J. Chapman and H. C. Foot, pp. 63–91.

Lalo, Charles. *Esthétique du rire.* Paris: Flammarion, 1949.

Lamennais, Félicité Robert de. *De l'art et du beau.* Paris, 1841.

La Rochefoucauld, François VI de Marcillac, duke of. *Maxims,* trans. Leonard Tancock. New York: Penguin, 1951.

Lauter, Paul, ed. *Theories of Comedy.* New York: Doubleday, 1964.

Ledoux, Joseph E., and William Hirst, eds. *Mind and Brain.* Cambridge: Cambridge University Press, 1986.

Levin, Harry. *Veins of Humor.* Cambridge: Harvard University Press, 1972.

Levine, Jacob. "Humour as a Form of Therapy." In *It's a Funny Thing,* ed. A. J. Chapman and H. C. Foot, pp. 127–37.

Loizos, Caroline. "Play Behaviour in Higher Primates: A Review." In *Primate Ethology,* ed. Desmond Morris. London: Weidenfeld and Nicolson, 1967, pp. 176–218.

Lorge, Dr. "Point de vue psychosomatique." In *Introduction à l'étude scientifique du rire,* ed. Dr. A. Berge et al., pp. 71–82.

Lucretius, Titus Carus. *The Way Things Are,* trans. Rolfe Humphries. Bloomington: Indiana University Press, 1968.

McFadden, George. *Discovering the Comic.* Princeton: Princeton University Press, 1982.

McGhee, Paul E. "Children's Humour: A Review of Current Research Trends." In *It's a Funny Thing,* ed. A. J. Chapman and H. C. Foot, pp. 199–209.

———. "A Model of the Origins and Early Development of Incongruity-Based Humour." In *It's a Funny Thing,* ed. A. J. Chapman and H. C. Foot, pp. 27–36.

———. "On the Cognitive Origins of Incongruity Humor: Fantasy Assimilation versus Reality Assimilation." In *The Psychology of Humor,* ed. J. Goldstein and P. McGhee, pp. 61–80.

———. "The Role of Arousal and Hemisphere Lateralization in Humor." In *Handbook of Humor Research,* ed. P. E. McGhee and J. H. Goldstein, 1:13–37.

McGhee, Paul, Paul E., and Jeffrey H. Goldstein. *Handbook of Humor Research.* 2 vols. New York: Springer-Verlag, 1983.

MacIntyre, Alasdair. *After Virtue.* Notre Dame, Ind.: University of Notre Dame Press, 1984.

Makarius, Laura. "Ritual Clowns and Symbolic Behaviour." *Diogenes* 69 (1970): 44–73.

Marquard, Odo. "Exile der Heiterkeit." In *Das Komische,* ed. W. Preisendanz and R. Warning, pp. 133–51.

Martineau, William H. "A Model of the Social Functions of Humor." In *The Psychology of Humor*, ed. J. Goldstein and P. McGhee, pp. 101–25.

Mast, Gerald. *The Comic Mind, Comedy and the Movies*. Chicago: University of Chicago Press, 1982.

Mehlman, Jeffrey. "How to Read Freud on Jokes: The Critic as Schadchen." *New Literary History* 6 (1975): 439–61.

Meredith, George. *An Essay on Comedy and the Uses of the Comic Spirit* [1877]. New York: Scribner's, 1897.

Milner, G. B. "Homo Ridens: Towards a Semiotic Theory of Humour and Laughter." *Semiotica* 5 (1972): 1–30.

Mindess, Harvey. *Laughter and Liberation*. Los Angeles: Nash, 1971.

Molière [Jean-Baptiste Poquelin]. *The Imaginary Invalid*, trans. John Wood. Baltimore: Penguin, 1959.

———. *The Misanthrope* and *Tartuffe*, trans. Richard Wilbur. New York: Harcourt, Brace, Jovanovich, 1965.

———. *Théâtre complet*, ed. Robert Jouanny. 2 vols. Paris: Garnier, n.d.

Monnier, A.-M. "Le mécanisme psycho-physiologique du rire." In *Introduction à l'étude scientifique du rire*, ed. Dr. A. Berge et al., pp. 61–62.

Monro, D. H. *Argument of Laughter*. Carlton, Victoria: Melbourne University Press, 1951.

Montaigne, Michel de. *The Complete Essays*, trans. Donald Frame. Stanford: Stanford University Press, 1965.

———. *Essais*, ed. P. Villey and V. Saulnier. Paris: Presses Universitaires de France, 1965.

Morris, Desmond, ed. *Primate Ethology*. London: Weidenfeld and Nicolson, 1967.

Nietzsche, Friedrich. *The Joyous Wisdom* [La Gaya Scienza]. New York: Macmillan, 1924. Vol. 10 of *The Complete Works*, trans. Th. Common. 18 vols.

———. *Thus Spake Zarathustra*. New York: Macmillan, 1924. Vol. 11 of *The Complete Works*, trans. Thomas Common. 18 vols.

Noguez, Dominique. "Structure du langage humoristique." *Revue d'Esthétique* 22 (1969): 33–54.

Olbrechts-Tyteca, Lucie. *Le comique du discours*. Brussels: Editions de l'Université de Bruxelles, 1968.

Olson, Elder. *The Theory of Comedy*. Bloomington: Indiana University Press, 1968.

Osborn, Kate, and Antony Chapman. "Suppression of Adult

Laughter: An Experimental Approach." In *It's a Funny Thing*, ed. A. J. Chapman and H. C. Foot, pp. 429–31.

Pascal, Blaise. *Les pensées*. Les Grands Ecrivains de la France. Paris: Hachette, 1921. Vol. 14.

——. *Pensées*, trans. A. J. Krailsheimer. Baltimore: Penguin, 1966.

——. *Les provinciales*. 1914. Vols. 4–7 of *Oeuvres*, ed. Léon Brunschvicg. 14 vols. 1908–21.

Paulos, John H. *Mathematics and Humor*. Chicago: University of Chicago Press, 1980.

Pickard-Cambridge, Arthur. *Dithyramb, Tragedy, and Comedy*. Oxford: Clarendon Press, 1966.

Pilcher, W. W. *The Portland Longshoremen*. New York: Holt, 1972.

Plaquevent, Jean. "Essai sur le rire chez l'enfant." In *Introduction à l'étude scientifique du rire*, ed. Dr. A. Berge et al., pp. 141–93.

Plato. *Politicus; Philebus; Ion*, trans. Harold N. Fowler. New York: Putnam, 1925.

——. *The Symposium*, trans. Suzy Q. Groden. Amherst: University of Massachusetts Press, 1970.

Pollio, Howard. "Notes toward a Field Theory of Humor." In *Handbook of Humor Research*, ed. P. E. McGhee and J. H. Goldstein, 1:213–30.

Preisendanz, Wolfgang, and Rainer Warning, eds. *Das Komische*. Munich: W. Fink, 1976.

Quintilianus, Marcus Fabius. *The Institutio Oratoria of Quintilian*, trans. H. E. Butler. 4 vols. Loeb Classical Library.

Rabelais, François. *Oeuvres complètes*. Bibliothèque de la Pléiade. Paris: Gallimard, 1965.

——. *The Portable Rabelais*, trans. Samuel Putnam. New York: Viking, 1946.

Radcliffe-Brown, A. R. "On Joking Relationships." *Africa* 13 (1940): 195–210; 19 (1949): 133–40.

Radin, Paul. *The Trickster: A Study in American Indian Mythology*. New York: Schocken, 1972.

Ramondt, Marie. *Studien über das Lachen*. Groningen: J. B. Wolters, 1962.

Revault d'Allonnes, Olivier. "Le comique, the comic, die Komik et la suite." *Revue d'Esthéthique* 19 (1966): 364–74.

Ribot, Théodore. *Théorie des sentiments*. Paris, 1899.

Ritter, Joachim. "Über das Lachen." *Blätter für Deutsche Philosophie* 14 (1940/41): 1–21.

Robinson, Vera. "Humor and Health." In *Handbook of Humor Research*, ed. P. E. McGhee and J. H. Goldstein, 2:109–28.

Sacks, Harvey. "Some Technical Considerations of a Dirty Joke." In *Studies in the Organization of Conversational Interaction*, ed. J. Schenkein. New York: Academic Press, 1978, 249–69.

Salameh, Waleed A. "Humor in Psychotherapy." In *Handbook of Humor Research*, ed. P. E. McGhee and J. H. Goldstein, 2:61–88.

Santayana, George. *Soliloquies in England—and Later Soliloquies*. New York: Scribner's Sons, 1922.

Saulnier, Claude. *Le sens du comique*. Paris: J. Vrin, 1940.

Schlegel, August Wilhelm. *Lectures on Dramatic Art and Literature* [1808], trans. J. Black. London, 1883.

Schmidt, Siegfried J. "Komik und Beschreibungsmodell kommunikativer Handlungsspiele." In *Das Komische*, ed. W. Preisendanz and P. Warning, pp. 165–89.

Schopenhauer, Arthur. *The World as Will and Representation*, trans. B. F. J. Payne. [1836–54]. 2 vols. New York: Dover, 1958.

Schwiech, Michel. "Réflexions sur le problème du rire." In *Introduction à l'étude scientifique du rire*, ed. Dr. A. Berge et al., pp. 123–34.

Shakespeare, William. *Twelfth Night*, ed. Charles T. Prouty. New York: Penguin, 1978.

Sherman, Lawrence. "Ecological Determinants of Gleeful Behaviours in Two Nursery School Environments." In *It's a Funny Thing*, ed. A. J. Chapman and H. C. Foot, pp. 357–60.

Socarides, Charles, ed. *The World of Emotions*. New York: International Universities Press, 1977.

Souriau, Etienne. "Le risible et le comique." *Journal de Psychologie* 41 (1949): 145–83.

Spencer, Herbert. "On the Physiology of Laughter" [1860]. In *Essays on Education and Kindred Subjects*. New York: E. P. Dutton, 1914, pp. 301–12.

Spinoza, Benedict de. *Ethics*, trans. R. H. M. Elwes. New York: Dover, 1951. Vol. 2 of *Works*. 2 vols. 1951.

Sroufe, L. A., and J. P. Wunsch. "The Development of Laughter in the First Year of Life." *Child Development* 43 (1972): 1326–44.

Stearns, Frederic R. *Laughing: Physiology, Pathophysiology, Psychology, Pathopsychology and Development*. Springfield, Ill.: Charles Thomas, 1972.

Stewart, Philip. "Les signes du comique." *Saggi e Ricerche di Letteratura Francese* 21 (1982): 191–241.

Stierle, Karlheinz. "Das Lachen als Antwort." In *Das Komische*, ed. W. Preisendanz and R. Warning, pp. 373–76.

Sully, James. *Essay on Laughter*. London: Longmans, Green, 1902.

Suls, Jerry. "Cognitive Processes in Humor Appreciation." In *Handbook of Humor Research*, ed. P. E. McGhee and J. H. Goldstein, 1:39–57.

Swabey, Marie Collins. *Comic Laughter*. New Haven: Yale University Press, 1961.

Todorov, Tzvetan. "Recherches sur le symbolisme linguistique, I: Le mot d'esprit et ses rapports avec le symbolique." *Poétique* 8 (1974): 215–45.

Torrance, Robert. *The Comic Hero*. Cambridge: Harvard University Press, 1978.

Twain, Mark [Samuel Clemens]. *The Adventures of Huckleberry Finn*. Toronto: Rinehart, 1948.

Voltaire [François-Marie Arouet]. *Candide*, trans. C. E. Merrill, Jr. New York: Random House, 1929.

———. *Dictionnaire philosophique*, ed. R. Naves. Paris: Garnier, 1967.

Walpole, Horace. "Thoughts on Comedy." [1775 and 1776]. London, 1798. Vol. 2 of *The Works of Horace Walpole*. 5 vols. 315–22.

Walsh, James. *Laughter and Health*. New York: D. Appleton, 1928.

Warning, Rainer. "Elemente einer Pragmasemiotik der Komödie." In *Das Komische*, ed. W. Preisendanz and R. Warning, pp. 279–333.

Wellershoff, Dieter. "Infantilismus als Revolt." In *Das Komische*, ed. W. Preisendanz and R. Warning, pp. 355–57.

Welsford, Enid. *The Fool: His Social and Literary History*. London: Faber and Faber, 1935.

Whitman, Cedric. *Aristophanes and the Comic Hero*. Cambridge: Harvard University Press, 1964.

Wieck, David Thoreau. "Funny Things." *Journal of Esthetics* 25 (1967): 437–47.

Willeford, William. *The Fool and His Scepter: A Study in Clowns and Jesters and Their Audience*. Chicago: Northwestern University Press, 1969.

Wimsatt, William Kurtz, ed. *The Idea of Comedy*. Englewood, N.J.: Prentice Hall, 1950.

Wolfenstein, Martha. *Children's Humour: A Psychological Analysis*. Glencoe, Ill.: Free Press, 1954.

Yerkes, Robert M. *The Great Apes*. New Haven: Yale University Press, 1929.

Index

Library of Congress Cataloging-in-Publication Data

Gutwirth, Marcel, 1923–
    Laughing matter : an essay on the comic / Marcel Gutwirth.
        p.   cm.
    Includes bibliographical references and index.
    ISBN 0-8014-2783-5
    1. Wit and humor—History and criticism.   2. Laughter.   3. Comic,
    The.   I. Title.
PN6147.G88   1993
801'.957—dc20   92-30520

211